How to Play
PICKLEBALL

The Complete Guide from A to Z

Illustrated Stroke Techniques
and Winning Strategies

Richard "Coach Mo" Movsessian
and
Joe Baker

How to Play Pickleball: The Complete Guide from A to Z

© 2018 Joseph H. Baker Jr. and Richard Movsessian

ISBN-13: 978-1-7239-9308-4

Interior and cover design by Sarah E. Holroyd
    (https://sleepingcatbooks.com)

CONTENTS

LIST OF FIGURES

ACKNOWLEDGEMENTS

Coach Mo and Joe Baker wish to thank and acknowledge the folks below who helped with this book project. These highly regarded pickleball players volunteered to review the manuscript and provide edits and guidance. Coach Mo and Joe Baker are responsible for any errors or issues remaining in the book.

Phil Bagley

Phil Bagley was born and raised in Massachusetts and resides in Florida. Phil and his partner Brian Staub won the "top prize at the top skill level at the top pickleball competition event" in 2013: the Gold Medal in the Men's Doubles open division at the USAPA National Tournament (The Sun City Festival), in Buckeye, Arizona. Phil continues to compete and teach workshops. He holds an IPTPA pickleball instructor certification. He is well known among the best of the best players. His record includes:

1. 2013 USAPA National Tournament Champion Men's Doubles Open with Brian Staub
2. 2012–2014 USAPA National Tournament 35+ Men's Doubles Champion with Brian Staub

3. 2014 USAPA National Tournament 35+ Mixed Doubles Champion with Jen Lucore
4. 2010 Nationals 35+ Men's Doubles Silver Medalist with Coach Mo
5. 2014 Tournament of Champions Men's Doubles Finalist with Brian Staub
6. 2014 USAPA National Tournament Men's Doubles Open Bronze Medal with Brian Staub
7. 2016 U.S. Open 45+ Men's Doubles Champion with Brian Staub.

Kathleen Wilcox

Before taking up pickleball two and a half years ago, Kathleen Wilcox was a 6.0-rated USPTA professional tennis player and club teaching professional. After retiring from the world of tennis, she got involved in pickleball. She quickly rose to become a 5.0-rated pickleball player. She has competed in the USAPA National Tournament (gold medal in Women's 50+ Singles, 4.5 skill level) and the U.S. Open. She was a "triple crown" gold medal winner in the 2018 Virginia State Senior games, winning gold in Women's Doubles, Mixed Doubles, and Singles.

Matty Klein

After retiring from the Los Angeles Police Department, Matty Klein moved to the Villages, Florida, and quickly developed his pickleball game. He has been teaching pickleball professionally for five years. He is an IPTPA certified pickleball instructor who frequently teaches pickleball alongside Coach Mo. Coach Matty has taught over 400 clinics and over 5,800 players across 18 states. Coach Matty also teaches on cruises and at various locations around the world with his wife, Coach Mei Shen. Matty's goal is to teach clinics and private lessons in all 50 states. Coach Matty also taught tennis and coached high school tennis.

PROLOGUE

Imagine This

Imagine this situation. As you step onto the court you see that your opponents are much younger, lighter, stronger, and more athletic than you and your partner. The situation is unsettling. "How can we possibly win?" you think. But one thing you know you have is a keen knowledge of pickleball strategy. You've read this book. You know what shot to hit in about every situation. You also know how to hit the most important and most difficult shots like the critical third shot.

The game begins. You stick to the method that you know works. Your opponents are indeed very fast. They display remarkable athletic skills. They hit hard and they scramble fast. However, your strategy is working. Ultimately you win and your opponents are left trying to figure out what went wrong. You feel great knowing that you put the basic principles to work.

This is not an unlikely scenario. Now over seventy-five years old, I beat guys half my age every day. So do many other folks. We do it by playing smart. We do it by playing high percentage pickleball.

The highlight of my pickleball career was in November, 2010 at the USAPA National Tournament held in Buckeye, Arizona. My partner, Phil Bagley, and I won the silver medal in the men's 35+ open doubles competition. Though my partner was younger, I was nearly seventy for this event. I was definitely the oldest in the 35+ bracket. I was certainly not the fastest or the most athletic among my competitors. How did we pull it off? Of course I had an exceptionally great partner, but the other reason is that we played smart, high percentage pickleball. We used the strategy and the techniques described in this book.

The only thing I like better than playing strategic pickleball is teaching it. When I'm not playing it, I'm teaching it. I'm eager to teach you. Are you ready to learn?

—Coach Mo

Where We All Begin: Hit It, Hit It!

When I was a kid, my mother had a badminton set. We put it up when we had friends over or when going to a cookout or camping outing. I loved this activity. We had enough racquets to outfit about eight players at a time. Once the game started we were continuously yelling, "Hit it, hit it!" Success was anything that could get the birdie back across the net. I carried on the tradition with my kids and I created another similar activity. I would inflate a large punch balloon and then outfit my kids and the neighborhood kids with badminton racquets. The object was to keep the balloon from ever hitting the ground. Once the first hit was made, a continuous chorus of "hit it, hit it" rang out. When I first stumbled onto a pickleball game, they lent me a wooden paddle and advised, "Just hit it over the net." So, in my first game, my newly acquainted partner and coach was yelling, "Hit it, hit it!" Fond memories were brought back and I was hooked immediately.

This simple two-word phrase, "hit it," summed up nicely both my technique and my strategy. Just like in childhood badminton, the only strategy I knew was to get it back across the net. My technique was to just hit it with whatever reaction my body produced.

I think that many folks coming to pickleball start out with the technique and strategy summed up by the phrase "hit it." In fact, I would say that at least half of all players just "hit it" or hit it to the weak opponent.

Fortunately, pickleball is really fun even if "hit it" is all you know. I certainly enjoyed pickleball even when "hit it" was all I knew how to do.

For some reason, as I've gotten older, I find that I get more serious about any endeavor I undertake. So, when I started playing pickleball, it wasn't long before I started getting serious and trying to learn how to become a better player. When I was in school, most of the sports required that you be big, tall, strong, or all of these to succeed. None of those words described me. Once I got involved in pickleball, I found out that, for once, I had a chance to be really good at a sport.

Because I had some table tennis and regular tennis in my background, I became a good intermediate pickleball player quickly. In fact, I was about the best banger in the social/recreational arena. I wanted more though. We had a group of top-notch tournament players in Richmond, Virginia, where I live. However, my skill was too low for this group. I could not get a clear recipe for what I needed to do to get to the level of the tournament players.

Then I heard that Coach Mo was coming to Richmond. I quickly scheduled private lessons with him. I had already compiled what I thought was the method needed to win. I also had a list of about a hundred questions on strategy and a stack of pre-printed court diagrams that could be used for creating strategy diagrams. Within a couple of hours, Coach Mo explained the whole story of pickleball strategy from A to Z. Within about six months I won my first silver medal in the 4.0+ skill division against some of the best senior tournament players in the area.

For some folks, getting serious and getting competitive will "take the fun out of it." For me, it's the opposite. The quest to get better and seeing it happen is exciting. So, I find that pickleball becomes even more enjoyable as my skill improves. A whole new "game within the game" opens up when all players get fully forward and begin working their strategies.

Hopefully this book will help you improve your skills and help further your enjoyment of the game.

—Joe Baker

CHAPTER 1: INTRODUCTION

What this Book is About

This book focuses on pickleball fundamentals and basic strategy. Specifically it focuses on shot techniques, player movement, player positioning, and how to play smart, high percentage pickleball.

Shot Technique

Shot technique is an often overlooked but critical key to success. Without good technique, you can make good shots sometimes, but you can't make good shots reliably.

A great analogy is in golf. Any golf pro will tell you that in golf, the key need is a great "short game," which means having great skill in getting the ball in or very close to the hole from a range of 50 yards or closer. So, the key need in the short game is precision shot placement, not power. In particular, the key need for each short game shot other than the final putt is distance control. So, the key need is to be able to "chip" the ball very close to the hole without the shot landing too short or too long. The only way to get a reliable chip shot is to have great technique.

Golfers with poor technique will usually find their ball further from the hole after making their chip shot than before making it. A golf professional is three times more likely to get "up and down" (get the ball in the hole in two shots) from fifty yards away as an "average Joe" golfer. Again, it is not strength or superior athletic ability that makes the difference; instead, it is technique.

The technique for just the chip shot alone requires a complete chapter in a typical book on golf. Every other shot in golf such as the pitch, the putt, the flop, and the bunker shot, has its own technique. So, in golf, many shot techniques are required. It is the same in pickleball.

Why all this talk about golf? The point is that technique can be complicated, but it is vitally important to achieving a high level of success. The same is true in tennis and in pickleball. In golf, the best players are not the biggest and strongest among the players. Instead, they are the players with the best technique. In pickleball, it's the same thing.

You may be thinking, "How difficult can hitting a wiffle ball be?" Indeed hitting it is not difficult, but hitting it in a way that reliably achieves the desired ball placement *is* really difficult. Even great tennis players must adjust to the difficulty of pickleball shot placement. When newcomers to pickleball play against experienced players, they usually do not get "beaten." Instead, they defeat themselves through a multitude of unforced errors caused by not being able to control the ball.

Just like in golf, in pickleball an important need is distance control. Let's look at some specific examples. With the serve and with the return of serve, deeper is better. However, too deep (going out of bounds) is terrible. Thus, the key need is distance control. With the third shot drop shot, the goal is to get the ball over the net but have it bounce in the kitchen. Again, this requires extremely good distance control. Even passing shots and hard drive shots must have distance control to avoid going out of bounds.

How do we achieve success? Just like in golf, the goal is to achieve a great setup and then execute a stroke that has the speed and technique to create the shot you are seeking. As the ball is in motion, the player must move to the ball to create the setup. Just like every shot in golf has its own technique, every shot in pickleball also has its own technique. In this book, we will explain all of these shot techniques.

A key theme of Coach Mo and this book is the vital importance of technique. Coach Mo repeats often, "When you have two players of equal athletic ability, the player with the best technique will win more often." Senior players with good technique usually defeat players half their age who are struggling to learn the required techniques.

Player Movement and Positioning

I can always spot a newcomer to the game, even if his or her shots are great. How? I can spot them by how they move and position themselves. They are usually doing way too much work, moving forward, then back, then forward again, etc. They are often even unsafe; it's like watching a fall that is about to happen. Their "home base" is exactly at the wrong place: right in the middle of "no man's land," the center of the service box.

In addition, newcomers "do their own thing." They worry only about their half of the court. They have a partner, but they are in no way partnered. They are not synchronized with their partner or connected to their partner. Even with great shot skill, their positioning would make them easy prey for any competent opponent. In this book, we will show you exactly where to be, how to move, and how to stay connected to your partner.

Strategy

Starting out, we intended this book to be about fundamentals and shot techniques. It quickly became apparent that it's hard to separate a discussion of technique and player positioning from a discussion of basic strategy. For example, why does it make sense to discuss the technique of the critical third shot, if you don't understand its purpose? And why does it make sense to discuss dinking if the player does not understand why and when to dink? So, this book discusses strategy basics along with fundamentals and shot techniques. For a complete treatment of pickleball strategy, refer to my other book, *At the Line Pickleball: The Winning Doubles Pickleball Strategy* by Joe Baker.

For newcomers to the game, a brief history of pickleball and a synopsis of the rules follow. If you already play pickleball and know how to keep score and change servers, skip ahead to Chapter 3.

CHAPTER 2: THE HISTORY AND BASIC RULES OF PICKLEBALL

Introduction

If you are already playing pickleball and know the main rules and how to keep score, you may wish to skip this chapter and move on to Chapter 3. This chapter is intended to help newcomers understand the basic rules and scoring system.

What is Pickleball?

Pickleball is a paddle sport that combines many elements of tennis, badminton, and table tennis. To describe it quickly with just one sentence, it is like miniature tennis that uses a badminton-sized court, the "old" badminton scoring system, a plastic wiffle ball, and a paddle that's about twice the size of a ping pong paddle. Whereas a standard tennis court, for doubles, measures 78 feet by 36 feet, a pickleball court measures 44 feet by 20 feet, exactly the same as a badminton court. As a standard basketball court is 94 feet by 50 feet, three pickleball courts can easily fit on one basketball court. The net and the rules for pickleball are very similar to those of tennis. The game can be played indoors or outdoors. Most indoor play involves setting up portable nets on a basketball court. The ideal situation for outdoor play is having courts designed specifically for pickleball. Another option is using part of a tennis court.

A Brief History

Pickleball was invented as a children's backyard pastime. The game started during the summer of 1965 on Bainbridge Island, Washington, at the home of former State Representative Joel Pritchard. He and two of his friends, Bill Bell and Barney McCallum, returned from golf and found their families bored one Saturday afternoon. They said their bored children were driving them nuts. They attempted to set up badminton, but no one could find the shuttlecock. They improvised with a wiffle ball and ping pong paddles. Their children were having fun immediately. Within a few days, they lowered the badminton net and fabricated paddles of plywood from a nearby shed. Pickleball caught on fast with their friends and neighbors. People began making their own paddles using jigsaws and marine plywood. Those who had access to badminton courts simply lowered the net. Others set up courts in their driveways and backyards, drawing lines with chalk. News of the fun new game spread by word of mouth. By the end of 1965, most of the rules were established.

The origin of the name, pickleball, is a bit of a mystery. It is thought to be derived from the name of the co-founder's Cocker Spaniel, Pickles, who would chase the ball and run off with it.

Characteristics of the Game

A key goal was to make the game fun and accessible for all ages and all family members. The founders wanted to avoid having player size and strength dominate the game. In tennis, a strong serve is vital and the serve is the most important shot of the game. About one third of the points scored in tennis come directly from the serve. So, in tennis, if you don't have a powerful serve, you cannot achieve much success.

In pickleball, the founders of the game specified that an underhand serve be used to avoid having serving strength dominate the game. In addition, the "two bounce rule" was designed to keep the serving team from attacking the net and the service return. The two bounce rule says that the serve must bounce before being hit and the return of serve must bounce before being hit. These two rules give the advantage to the receiving team, which can return the serve and attack the net, not the serving team, which must wait for the return of serve to bounce. The seven-foot non-volley zone near the net has two purposes. First, it prevents a team from "building a wall" directly at the net that enables easy "spiking." Second, the non-volley zone provides a "safe place" for a team trying to approach the net to place their shot. As a result of these game design features and the compact court, young and old players and male and female players are on a much more even footing in pickleball than in tennis, where strength and extreme mobility are essential even at the 4.0 skill level. Compared to tennis, pickleball success is driven more by ball placement capability and strategy than by strength and quickness. And, compared to tennis, pickleball success is driven more by eliminating errors than by trying to generate winners.

Please don't mistake this to mean that strength, power, mobility, and quickness have no importance in pickleball. It's nearly impossible to compete at the 5.0 skill level in pickleball without having speed, mobility, and put-away power in addition to great technique and strategy.

Another aspect of pickleball is the extreme social nature of the game compared to tennis. In doubles tennis, you stick with your partner and your opponent with his or her partner through the duration of a match that can last hours. In pickleball, a game usually lasts 15 minutes. At the conclusion of a doubles pickleball game, you typically "mix it up" and play with a new partner. The compact court also promotes player interaction.

The Basic Rules of Doubles Pickleball

The Pickleball Serve

As with tennis, badminton, and table tennis, the game and each rally begin with a serve. The underhand serve is made diagonally, starting with the right-hand service square and alternating from the right-hand side of the court to the left-hand side of the court as long as the server holds the serve. The receiving team does not alternate positions. To avoid fault, the serve must clear the seven-foot non-volley zone in front of the net and land in the service court diagonally opposite the server.

In tennis, the server is allowed two serve attempts. In pickleball, each server is allowed only one serve attempt. At the start of each new game, the first serving team is allowed only one fault before giving up the ball to the opponents. Thereafter both members of each doubles team serve until faulting, at which time the ball is turned over to the opposing team. The team member serving the second serve, after the first server's team faults, must serve from whatever side the second server is playing from. When the receiving team wins the serve, the player in the right-hand court always serves first. A service fault occurs if the served ball touches any area outside of the correct service box or if the served ball goes into the net.

The serving team's point score will always be an even number when the serving team's starting server is serving on the right-hand side of the court. A team's score will always be an odd number when their team's starting server is serving from the left-hand side of the court.

Players may toss a coin or rally the ball until a fault is made to determine the opening server. The winner of the toss/rally has the option of serving first or receiving first.

Scoring

Pickleball uses the "old" scoring system of badminton, which was in effect when pickleball was invented. Most newcomers to the game find the scoring system and the sequence of serving to be extremely confusing. It does take a while to learn how to keep score and how to switch servers and serving positions. Had the game been invented by folks who were not badminton players, I think the scoring system would use rally point scoring, in which the winner of a rally scores a point regardless of who serves. The modern badminton scoring system uses rally point scoring.

The pickleball scoring system operates as follows. A team can only score points when serving. Both members of each doubles team serve until faulting before the ball is turned over to the opposing team. This is called a Side Out. So each team has a first server and a second server.

Recall from above that at the start of each new game, the first serving team is allowed only one fault before giving up the ball to the opponents (a side out).

The game is played to 11 points; however, a team must win by 2 points. It's not uncommon for many side outs to occur in a row with no points being earned.

In Figure 2-1, you can see that after a fault is made by the receiving team, and a point is scored by the serving team, the serving team's players switch positions on the court and the same player continues to serve. When the serving team makes its first fault, the serving team's players stay in their same court positions (not switching sides), and the second partner then serves. When they make their second fault, they stay in their same court positions, and turn the ball over to the other team. So, players switch between the left and right side of the court only when they score.

Rally	Score	Server (Circled)	Rally Winner	Result	Outcome/Comments
1	0-0-2	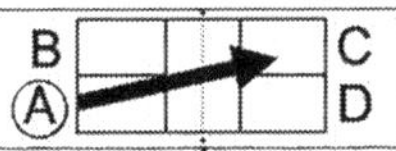 B ⟶ C / (A) ⟶ D	A&B	Point	Unforced Error (UE) by player D. Dink flub into net.
2	1-0-2	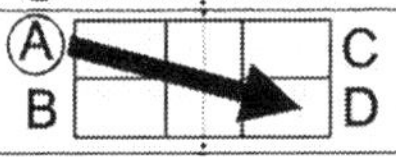 (A) ⟶ C / B ⟶ D	A&B	Point	Weak, short return of serve by David. Down the middle drive winner by Amy.

Figure 2-1 Serving team members switch positions after they score

The sequence for announcing the score is as follows: serving team's score first, opponents score second, and server number third. So if the server calls the score 5-4-1, the serving team has 5 points, the opposing team has 4 points, and server number 1 is serving. At the very start of the game, the score is called out 0–0-2, which means each team has zero points and only the second serve remains. Remember, at the start of each new game, the first serving team is allowed only one fault before giving up the ball to the opponents. So, in a sense, the game starts with the second serve.

The Return of the Serve and the Two Bounce Rule

When the ball is served, the receiving team must let it bounce before returning it. Likewise the serving team must allow the return of serve shot to bounce before returning it. Thus with the first two shots of the game, the serve and the return of serve, the ball must bounce before being hit. This is called the double bounce rule. To avoid fault, the return of serve shot must clear the net and not go out of bounds.

Subsequent Shots

After the ball has bounced once in each team's court, both teams may either volley the ball (hit the ball before it bounces) or play it off a bounce (ground stroke).

The Non-Volley Zone (NVZ)

The NVZ is the court area within seven feet of the net on both sides of the net. Volleying is prohibited within the NVZ. This rule prevents players from executing smashes or spikes from a position within the zone. It is a fault if, when volleying a ball, the player steps in the NVZ, including on the NVZ boundary line. A player may legally be in the NVZ any time other than when volleying a ball. Although a player may legally be in the NVZ any time other than when volleying a ball, it is not wise to step into the NVZ except when necessary to reach a ball that has bounced. Here's why. If you are in the NVZ, a smart opponent will hit a rather fast shot directly at you. You will not have time to establish yourself outside the NVZ to return such a shot, and if you touch the ball before it has bounced, it will be a fault. So, smart players step into the NVZ only when necessary to return a ball that has bounced and then get back out of the NVZ as soon as possible after making the return. The NVZ is commonly referred to as "the kitchen."

Basic Doubles Strategy

In a nutshell, the best doubles pickleball strategy is to get your team fully forward at the non-volley zone line (NVZ line) as quickly as possible while trying to keep your opponents as far away from the net as possible for as long as possible. Having both doubles team members fully forward at the NVZ line is both the best offensive positioning and best defensive positioning. All top players seek to play parallel with their partner and as far forward on the court as possible—in other words, all the way up to the NVZ boundary line. So, the team receiving the serve returns the serve and scrambles forward to the NVZ line before the serving team sends back the third shot of the game. After the serve is returned (the second shot of the game), the serving team is now facing opponents who are fully forward at the NVZ line. The most frequent "third shot" (i.e., the shot after the return of serve shot) strategy is for the serving team to place a softly hit drop shot into the kitchen. Such a slow shot allows the serving team to scramble forward to the NVZ line. With all players fully forward, the best strategy is to keep the ball very low so that it cannot be smashed or volleyed. In other words, the strategy at this point is to avoid giving your opponents an attackable shot. So, players may "dink" the ball back and forth rather than doing anything that could get the ball too high. A dink shot is a softly hit shot, sometimes just a tap, which seeks to drop the ball over the net so that it lands in the kitchen. Just like in table tennis, as soon as a mistake is made that causes the ball to get high, a put-away smash will likely occur.

A Typical Example Game

The two players on Team 1 are Amy (A) and Beth (B). The two players on Team 2 are Chad (C) and David (D).

0–0-Start, (Usually called "0–0-2"), Rally #1, Amy Serving from Right Side

Amy wins the coin toss and she elects to serve first. Amy calls out the score: 0–0-2. She serves diagonally from the right side to Chad and her underhand serve lands in the correct serving box (good serve). Chad returns the serve toward Beth with a low lob that gives him time to run up to the NVZ line before Beth can hit the ball back. So Chad rushes forward to be alongside his partner, David, who has been fully forward since Amy made her serve. Beth waits for this lob-like return of serve to bounce (the two bounce rule), and then she hits a soft, rather slow drop shot into the kitchen near David's backhand. Amy and Beth see that the soft drop shot will land and bounce in the kitchen and so they both rush forward to the NVZ line. David tries to make a sharp crosscourt dink shot but his shot goes into the net, ending the rally. Team 1 scores a point. Figure 2-2 below shows the starting score, player arrangement, result, and outcome/comments.

Rally	Score	Server (Circled)	Rally Winner	Result	Outcome/Comments
1	0-0-2	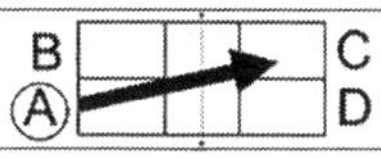 B ➝ C / (A) D	A&B	Point	Unforced Error (UE) by player D. Dink flub into net.

Figure 2-2 Starting score, player arrangement, result

1–0-2, Rally #2, Amy Serving from Left Side

Amy and Beth swap courts but their opponents do not swap courts. Amy calls out the score: 1–0-2. Amy serves diagonally from the left side to David and her underhand serve lands in the correct serving box (good serve). David returns the serve to Amy's strong forehand, but his return is weak and short. Amy waits for this return of serve to bounce (the two bounce rule). She sees a rather wide gap between Chad and David as David is approaching the net and she places a fast forehand shot directly between them, being careful not to overpower the shot and potentially send it out of bounds. The shot works perfectly. Neither Chad nor David reaches the shot and the shot stays in bounds, ending the rally with a point scored for Team 1. The box below shows the starting score, player arrangement, result, and outcome/comments.

Rally	Score	Server (Circled)	Rally Winner	Result	Outcome/Comments
2	1-0-2	 (A) ➝ C / B D	A&B	Point	Weak, short return of serve by David. Down the middle drive winner by Amy.

Figure 2-3 Starting score, player arrangement, result

2–0-2, Rally #3, Amy Serving from Right Side

Amy and Beth swap courts but their opponents do not swap courts. Amy calls out the score: 2–0-2. Note that the serving team's score is an even number when Amy, the starting server, is serving from the right side as she is now. Amy serves diagonally from the right side to Chad and her underhand serve hits the top of the net but lands in the correct service box. Chad calls out, "Let." A serve is called a let when the ball hits the net cord but still lands in the service court. Such a serve is not considered a fault and the server must repeat the service attempt. So, Amy repeats her serve attempt to Chad and her underhand serve lands in the correct service box. Chad returns the serve toward Amy with a low lob. Chad rushes forward to join his partner at the NVZ line. Amy waits for this lob-like return of serve to bounce (the two bounce rule), and then she attempts to hit a drop shot into the kitchen near David's backhand. Her shot is too high, allowing David to volley the shot back toward Amy's left foot while she is caught in "no man's land," the area between the baseline and the NVZ line. Amy makes a second drop shot attempt into the kitchen and is successful. She follows this shot forward and she and her partner make it to the NVZ line. Neither team sees an offensive opportunity. So, all players just dink the ball over the net, trying to keep the ball low and "unattackable." After a few dink exchanges, Amy hits a dink shot that goes into the net. Neither team scores a point.

Rally	Score	Server (Circled)	Rally Winner	Result	Outcome/Comments
3	2-0-2	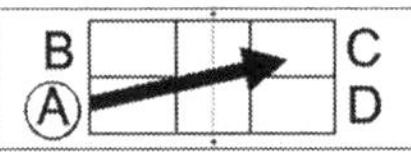 B → C (A) D	C&D	Side-Out	Unforced Error (UE) by player A. Dink flub into net.

Figure 2-4 Starting score, player arrangement, result

Side Out

As they do not score a point here, Amy and Beth do not swap sides. Neither do Chad or David. At the start of each new game, the first serving team is allowed only one fault before giving up the ball to the opponents. So, it is "side out," and the serve transfers to the team of Chad and David.

0–2-1, Rally #4, Chad Serving from Right Side

At the start of the game and following each side out, the serve always begins from the right side. Chad calls the score: 0–2-1. Chad serves diagonally from the right side to Amy and his underhand serve lands in the correct serving box (good serve). Amy uses a semi-lob and returns the serve toward Chad. Amy rushes forward to join her partner at the NVZ line. Chad waits for this lob-like return of serve to bounce (the two bounce rule), and then he attempts to hit a fastball drive toward Beth. Beth sees that the ball is very fast and nearly at the height of her shoulders. She chooses not to hit the ball and watches it fly out of bounds, ending the rally. No point is scored from the rally.

Rally	Score	Server (Circled)	Rally Winner	Result	Outcome/Comments
4	0-2-1	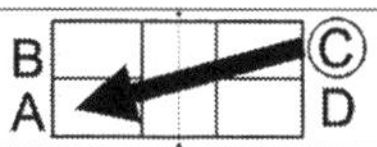 B C A D	A&B	Switch Server	Unforced Error (UE) by player C. Third shot drive attempt goes out of bounds deep.

Figure 2-5 Starting score, player arrangement, result

0–2-2, Rally #5, Serve Passes from Chad to David, David Serving from Left Side

As no point was scored, Chad and David do not switch courts and neither do Amy and Beth. All players are in their original positions. After this first server fault, the serve now passes from Chad to David. David calls out the score: 0–2-2. David serves diagonally from the left side to Beth and his underhand serve lands in the correct serving box (good serve). Beth returns the serve toward David with a soft, deep shot. Beth rushes forward to get alongside her partner at the NVZ line. David waits for this floating return of serve to bounce (the two bounce rule), and then he hits a nice drop shot into the kitchen near Beth's backhand. Chad and David see that the soft drop shot will land and bounce in the kitchen and so they both rush forward to the NVZ line. Seeing no holes or gaps in the defense and seeing no other good options, Beth dinks the ball crosscourt into the kitchen toward David. David returns the dink shot crosscourt to Beth. This back and forth crosscourt exchange between Beth and

David continues until Beth gets drawn out wide to a sideline and fails to move back toward the middle following her return. This leaves a hole and David sends a great "down the middle" shot through the hole that is not returned, ending the rally. Team 2 scores a point.

Rally	Score	Server (Circled)	Rally Winner	Result	Outcome/Comments
5	0-2-2	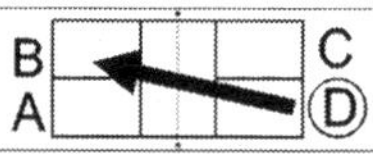 B C A (D)	C&D	Point	Beth drawn out wide during dinking, leaves a hole. Down the middle winner by David.

Figure 2-6 Starting score, player arrangement, result

1–2-2, Rally #6, David Serving from Right Side

As they have scored a point, Chad and David swap courts but their opponents do not swap courts. David calls out the score: 1–2-2. David serves diagonally from the right side to Amy and his underhand serve hits the top of the net and falls onto the NVZ line. However, the NVZ line is part of the kitchen, not part of the service box. This serve is a fault, not a let, since the serve did not go into the correct service box. This ends the rally. No point is scored in this rally.

Note that a ball that touches any part of the service box lines except the NVZ line is considered good (in the box). The service area center line belongs to both service courts.

Rally	Score	Server (Circled)	Rally Winner	Result	Outcome/Comments
6	1-2-2	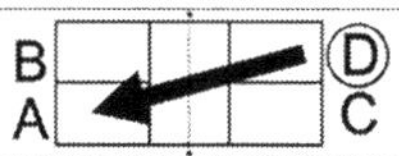 B (D) A C	A&B	Side-Out	Unforced Error (UE) by David. Service Fault.

Figure 2-7 Starting score, player arrangement, result

Side Out

As both members of the doubles team served until faulting, it is side out and the serve is turned over to the Amy/Beth team. As they do not score a point here, Chad and David do not swap sides. Neither do Amy or Beth.

2–1-1, Rally #7, Amy Serving from Right Side

As Amy is on the right side, she starts serving even though she was the last to serve on her team. Amy calls out the score: 2–1-1. Note that she was the first server on her team and that her score will always be an even number when she is serving from the (original) right side. Amy and Beth are in their original positions, but Chad and David are opposite their original positions.

Amy serves diagonally from the right side to David and her underhand serve lands in the correct serving box (good serve). David returns the serve toward Amy with a rather high lob. David rushes forward to join Chad at the NVZ line. Amy waits for this lob-like return of serve to bounce (the two bounce rule), and then she hits a nice drop shot into the kitchen near Chad's backhand. Amy and Beth see that the soft drop shot will land and bounce in the kitchen and so they both rush forward to the NVZ line. Chad sees that Amy and Beth are tightly linked and they are guarding his sideline. Seeing no good options, Chad hits a crosscourt dink to Beth's backhand. This back and forth crosscourt dink exchange between Beth and Chad goes on for a while. Though they are left out of the hitting exchange, Amy and David are staying engaged, moving with the ball, and watching like hawks for an opportunity to poach any crosscourt dink exchange shot that can be reached. After a while, Chad gets impatient and attempts an offensive lob over Amy's left shoulder. The lob is weak and too short. Amy calls "take it" to her partner, Beth, since Beth can hit it rather hard with her forehand. Beth smashes the ball down the middle for an easy put away. This ends the rally, with Team 1 scoring a point.

Rally	Score	Server (Circled)	Rally Winner	Result	Outcome/Comments
7	2-1-1	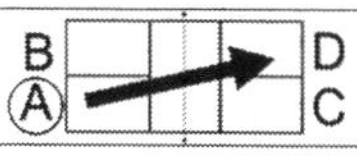 B → D Ⓐ C	A&B	Point	Bad lob by Chad, very short. Smash winner by Beth.

Figure 2-8 Starting score, player arrangement, result

3–1-1, Rally #8, Amy Serving from Left Side

Since they scored a point, Amy and Beth swap courts but their opponents do not swap courts. Amy calls out the score: 3-1-1. Amy serves diagonally from the left side to Chad and her underhand serve lands in the correct serving box (good serve). Chad returns the serve toward Amy using a rather fast, low shot. Chad starts moving forward to join David at the NVZ line. Amy waits for this return of serve to bounce (the two bounce rule). Amy notices that Chad is slow in getting forward. So, she hits a drop shot that bounces near David's left foot. This soft drop shot allows Amy and Beth to rush forward to the NVZ line. Chad manages to get the ball back over the net but it is a "pop up," allowing Amy an easy forehand smash shot. Unfortunately she overpowers and misaims the smash and her shot goes out of bounds deep, ending the rally. No point is scored.

Rally	Score	Server (Circled)	Rally Winner	Result	Outcome/Comments
8	3-1-1	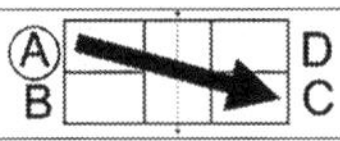 (A) → D / B C	C&D	Switch Server	Unforced Error (UE) by Amy. Smash went out of bounds deep.

Figure 2-9 Starting score, player arrangement, result

3–1-2, Rally #9, Serve Passes to Beth, Beth Serving from Right Side

As no point was scored, nobody switches courts. No player is in their original starting position. After this first server fault, the serve now passes from Amy to Beth. Beth calls out the score: 3–1-2. Beth serves diagonally from the right side to David and her underhand serve lands in the correct serving box (good serve). David returns the serve toward Beth with a soft, floating shot. David rushes forward to join Chad at the NVZ line. Beth waits for this lob-like return of serve to bounce (the two bounce rule), and then she hits a nice drop shot into the kitchen near Chad's backhand. Amy and Beth see that the drop shot attempt is not looking good. It is too high and Chad will be able to volley it back with good speed. So, Amy and Beth do not charge forward; instead they stay deep and they get compressed in a "split step" position. Chad's shot is directed near Beth's left heel. Beth manages to return the shot, fortunately getting it to land in the kitchen near Chad. As soon as Amy and Beth see that the shot will likely bounce in the kitchen, they quickly scramble forward to the NVZ line. Chad sees that Amy and Beth are tightly linked and they are guarding his sideline. Seeing no good options, Chad hits a crosscourt dink to Amy's backhand. Amy eventually flubs and hits the ball into the net. This ends the rally. No point is scored.

Rally	Score	Server (Circled)	Rally Winner	Result	Outcome/Comments
9	3-1-2	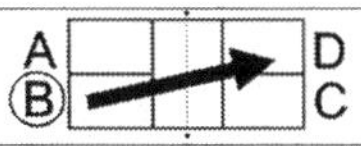 A ——▶ D (B) C	C&D	Side-Out	Unforced Error (UE) by Player A (Amy). Dink flub into net.

Figure 2-10 Starting score, player arrangement, result

Side Out

As both members of the doubles team served until faulting, it is side out and the serve is turned over to the Chad/David team. Since no point was scored, nobody changes positions. No player is in their original starting position.

1–3-1, Rally #10, David Serving from Right Side

As David is on the right side, he starts serving even though he was the last to serve on his team. David calls out the score: 1–3-1. Note that since the starting server (Chad) is on the left side instead of the right side, their score will be an odd number (and it is, their score is 1).

I think from the above, you can grasp the scoring system and serve sequencing system. Indeed it is confusing to the beginner. However, after a few outings, you will know the system well. But, after a long rally, even experienced players can have trouble remembering who served the ball and whether the server was the first or second server.

CHAPTER 3: THE GRIP

Most coaches recommend, and most good players use, one grip for all shots: the Continental grip. Here's how to do it. With the paddle blade vertical (straight up and down), grip the handle as if gripping a hammer. If you were to hammer with the edge of your paddle, this is

Continental Paddle Grip

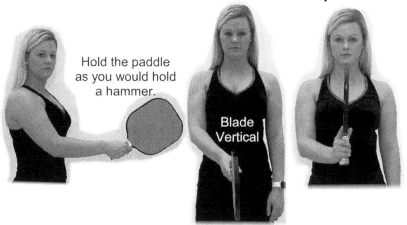

Figure 3-1 The Continental grip

how you would grip the paddle. Some folks also call it a trigger grip. See Figure 3–1.

Here's how to check that it's right. Your thumb and the rest of your hand should form a V on the top of the paddle handle (see Figure 3–2). An easy check before each rally is to extend your hand as if ready to chop with a hatchet and ensure the paddle blade is straight up and down. As pickleball action is rather fast, the grip you start with will likely be the grip you have at the end of each rally. So, don't start with a bad grip.

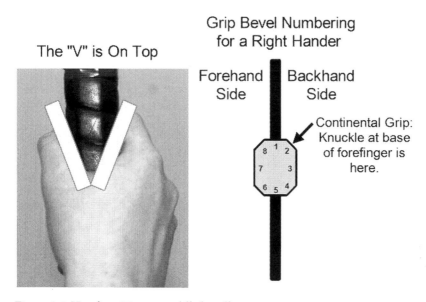

Figure 3-2 Hand position on paddle handle

Most coaches suggest, and most good players agree, that you should not make any grip adjustments during play. The Continental grip serves well for all forehand and backhand shots. In advanced play, most pickleball shots occur near the net. In such close range exchanges, there is no time for making adjustments or switching grips.

Tennis players often switch grips between forehand and backhand ground stroke shots in order to use an optimal grip for each. Indeed, the

Figure 3-3 The neutral Continental grip gives natural, equal upward hits for backhand and forehand shots

Continental grip is a "compromise" grip, not perfect for forehand shots or for backhand shots, but is, instead, the best "one grip solution" for all shots. If you rotate your hand slightly clockwise (when looking at the butt of the paddle) to slightly improve forehand performance, you then degrade backhand performance, and vice-versa.

Most coaches advise to practice with and "work in" the Continental grip until you no longer feel any urge to change away from it. A good practice drill is to hit alternating forehand and backhand volleys against a practice wall. You obviously can't change the grip between hits. After a short period of getting used to it, you will realize that the Continental grip is the right way to go.

Another advantage of the Continental grip is that it gives a natural upward hit for both backhand and forehand shots. Here's why. When playing correctly, you should be hitting the ball slightly in front of your body. Thus, your forearm is slightly angled up (toward your body). If your grip is correct, this should also angle the paddle up.

A personal preference of mine is to hold the paddle not near the end of the handle but as far up and close to the face as possible. I also lay my pointer finger on the paddle face. I feel this provides the most definite feel for where the center of the paddle is and what angle the paddle is facing.

To the extent possible, the free hand (i.e., the non-paddle hand), should touch the paddle after every shot to improve steadiness, control, and paddle face aiming. If a right-handed player keeps his left hand on the paddle, his left hand knows where the center of the paddle is located and this helps when turning the shoulders to set up the aim point. Coach Mo suggests placing the tip of the middle finger of the left hand at the center of the paddle "sweet spot" (see Figure 3-4).

As far as grip pressure goes, you certainly do not need a death grip, but you can't allow the paddle to slip or have the face deflect in the event of an off-center hit. What's really important for about every shot in pickleball is that wrist action be eliminated. The wrist should stay firm.

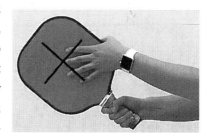

Figure 3-4 The paddle sweet spot

Common Mistakes

1. **Favoring the forehand hit.** It appears to me that most social players are not using the Continental grip, but instead a grip rotated slightly to the right that favors forehand shots. So, they optimize their forehand shots but concede their backhand shots because it's difficult to make good backhand shots using a forehand grip. Breaking such a habit and making a permanent adoption of the Continental grip is a huge change and it could degrade your game for a while before it improves it. I know that minor changes to the golf grip and swing can make your scores worse for a long time before such changes get you to a better place. However, you will

never become a great player if you use a grip that leads either to a weak backhand or to a weak forehand. Per Coach Mo: a doubles team is only as strong as the weakest player's weakest shot. When I see a player using a forehand grip, all I have to do is hit a shot or two to their backhand to win the rally.

2. **Using the handshake grip.** A handshake grip yields the eastern forehand grip, which favors forehand shots but is weak for backhand shots. For a right-handed player, the handshake grip puts the V of the hand not on the top, but slightly on the right of the paddle handle.

Making it Happen

You can't just read about the grip and expect it to happen. Here's your homework assignment.

1. Find a "practice wall," that is, any wall you can hit the ball against, and practice in the Continental grip. A great drill is to hit alternating forehand and backhand shots. An even better drill is to hit alternating forehand and backhand volleys against a practice wall. You obviously can't change the grip between volley hits.

2. When you go out to play pickleball, before each rally, hold your paddle out like you are holding a hatchet, and make sure the blade is vertical (straight up and down).

CHAPTER 4: THE SERVE

Basic Rules of the Serve

The serve must be made with an underhand stroke so that contact with the ball is made below waist level. Waist level is defined as the level of the navel. The definition of underhand is strict. Specifically, the arm must be moving in an upward arc and all of the paddle head must be below the wrist when it strikes the ball.

You may not serve the ball from a bounce. Instead, the ball must be struck before it hits the playing surface. The serve must get into the correct service box or else it is a fault. So, the ball must clear the net and the NVZ line and land in the opponent's crosscourt (diagonally opposite court) service box. The serve is good if it lands on any service box boundary line except the NVZ line. Note that a short serve that lands in the kitchen or on the NVZ line is a fault. The NVZ line (the whole thickness of it) is part of the non-volley zone (the kitchen).

At the beginning of the serve, the server must have both feet behind the baseline. At the time the ball is struck, at least one foot must be on the ground behind the baseline and the server's feet may not touch the playing surface in an area outside of the behind-the-baseline serving area. The behind-the-baseline serving area is defined as the area behind the baseline and on or between the imaginary lines extended from the court centerline and each sideline. So, when serving, you cannot step onto the court until after your paddle makes contact with the ball.

Serve Technique

For some reason, many otherwise great players struggle with the serve. Once their confidence is shaken, the struggle worsens. I think if you follow the suggestions below, you can end any struggles you may have.

Develop a Pre-Serve Routine

All great golfers and tennis players have a pre-shot routine where they set up for success and for a smooth and continuous journey toward making the strike. If you watch the professional tennis players on the Tennis Channel you will see that the pre-serve routine is extremely consistent from serve to serve. The following is a suggested routine.

1. Set your feet. I use a stance that is roughly square to my opponent. However, many top players use other variations.
2. Bounce the ball a few times. Most tennis players do this.
3. Call the score, ensure your opponent is ready, and spot your target, for example, dead center of the service box. Talking or calling the score while serving can distract you and cause faults.
4. While holding the ball against the center of the paddle, visualize a ball flight path that provides a very generous clearance above the net. Rotate your wrist to the right (for

Figure 4-1 Focus and visualize the ball flight path

a right-handed player) to enable having the paddle face aimed at (square to) the target flight path.

5. Draw the paddle back while attempting to keep the face from shifting left or right of the target.

6. Hold the ball from above and drop it as you swing the paddle forward, trying to keep the paddle face always pointing to the ball flight path.

7. Once you serve, make sure you quickly get back into ready position behind the baseline.

Like the tennis pros, try to avoid any hesitations or variance. If any interruption occurs, go back to Step 2 above. Usually when I have a service fault, I realize that I was not disciplined in following the routine.

Many players use a serve where they step across the baseline when serving. It is perfectly okay to step into this shot. If you do this, you should get back behind the baseline in time to judge the return of serve shot, which could come to you very deep. Neither member of the serving team should be inside the baseline until after the return of serve shot has been evaluated. It's nearly impossible to hit a great third shot if you are retreating while trying to hit it. It's much easier to travel into the court than to travel out.

Some of the service swing comes from the weight shift toward the lead foot or the stepping out, some of the movement comes from upper torso rotation, and some comes from the shoulder. The arm moves like a pendulum from the shoulder. The movement is very similar to a straight bowling ball release.

I see many social players use a very quick swatting action that uses wrist action. Though many folks are successful with this, I would never recommend it. Instead, I think it's best to minimize paddle face rotation and curving at the moment of impact. This can be achieved by reducing wrist and elbow action and letting the swing come from the torso and shoulder.

To some extent, you can "groove in" your routine in your home, even if you have no practice wall. Just go through the steps and pretend to make a strike. If you have access to a gymnasium or tennis practice wall, you can practice your serve using a wall. You can use easy-to-remove painter's tape to mark the top of an imaginary net and a target spot. Otherwise you can practice on an empty pickleball court.

Photos

The following photographs illustrate some key points.

The Serve: Aiming the Paddle

Key Points: 1) Spot the target and aim the paddle face. Rotate the wrist and lock it in place. 2) The "swing" will come from the shoulder as the arm moves like a pendulum. 3) The back is bent. 4) Drop the ball from above and keep watching through contact. A mistake is to look up (or peek) too soon. 5) Step into the shot with the left foot. 6) The non-paddle hand drops the ball and then stays out for balance.

The Serve: Contact

Key Points: 1) Keep the paddle face aimed at the target trajectory. 2) Drop the ball from above. Afterwards, the hand moves toward the target for balance. 3) Watch the ball make contact with the paddle. 4) Make a sound at the exact moment of contact to ensure you are watching the ball make contact. 5) You may step onto the court after contact. If you do step onto the court, get back behind the line before the return of serve is made.

The Serve
Aiming the Paddle

Figure 4-2 The serve: aiming the paddle

The Serve
Contact

The Serve
Follow Through

Figure 4-3 The serve: contact   *Figure 4-4 The serve: follow through*

The Serve: Follow Through

Key Points: 1) Keep the paddle face on line. Think about pushing the ball along the desired trajectory line. 2) Keep your head down until well after contact. 3) If you follow through completely and properly, you should be able to kiss your serving arm bicep at the end of the full follow through.

A Good Way to Learn How to Serve

A good way to minimize failure and immediately build confidence with serving is as follows. Instead of standing behind the baseline, stand very close to the net. See Figure 4-5. You might think this is so easy that it's ridiculous. However, I urge you to follow the system.

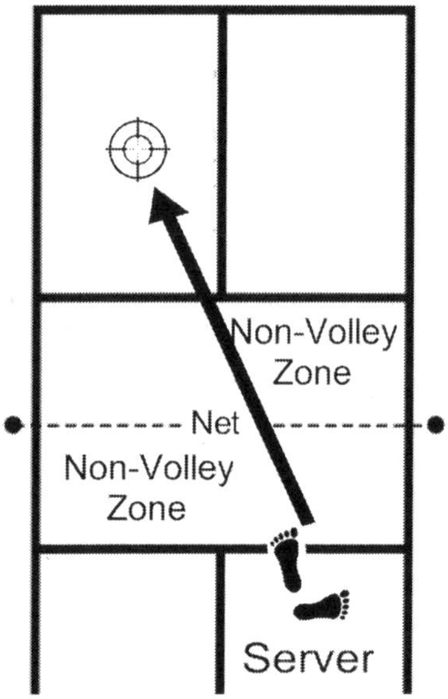

1. Use your complete pre-shot routine for every serve. Your aim point should be dead center of the service box. The ball flight path should clear the net by at least two feet. This gives you enough leeway for error.

2. Execute the serve and note the landing spot.

3. Repeat this until the ball is consistently landing in the middle of the box. Once you can get 10 in a row into the center of the box, move back a couple of feet.

4. Repeat the above until you can get 10 in a row into the center of the box, then move back a couple of feet.

Figure 4-5 Start out close to the net and aim for the center of the box

5. Repeat the above. At some point you may start faulting. If so, go back closer and continue practicing. You may need several practice sessions before you groove in a consistent serve.

Do not just hit the ball in the general direction of the service box. Instead, choose an exact target, visualize the exact trajectory you desire, and think about having the paddle face push the ball along the trajectory path.

You can also use a practice wall to develop your serving skill. Again, start close to ensure success, and then work further away.

Serving Strategy Discussion

Like lobbing, serving is another subject that creates many arguments. Most players are social/recreational players, not tournament players. In the social arena of intermediate players, a serve that is fast, spinning, deep, and placed at the backhand indeed trips up players. I have such a weapon, and indeed I can sometimes win several consecutive points in a row from my serve alone. Yes, it has a higher risk of faulting than a plainer serve, but I know, in the social arena, it wins more points than it loses.

However I rarely play in the social arena. Instead, I desire to play against the strongest opponents that will allow me to join them. In this arena, my serving tricks cost me more points than I gain.

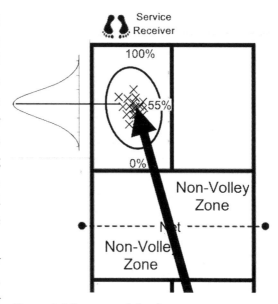

Figure 4-6 Serves made by the pros, on average, land at only 55 percent of the service box depth

I have studied thousands of pickleball rallies via slow motion video to see what works, what does not, and what the top pros do to win matches. I do not find that the top professionals serve deep or that they try to hit backhands or sidelines. Instead I find that their serves, on average, go right to the center of the box. Specifically, on average, their serves land at only 55–60 percent of the service box depth. See Figure 4-7. I do not find that they try to hit backhands or baselines, but instead I find that they use rather plain serves. Further, as service faults and service return faults are so infrequent, I do not find that "super serves," when used, have a significant bearing on the outcome of advanced level play.

With about every type of shot in pickleball, there's a tradeoff between the benefits of aggression (the additional rallies won) and the penalties of aggression (the additional rallies lost due to aggression, perhaps from shots going into the net or out of bounds—see Figure 4-7). The shape of the curve

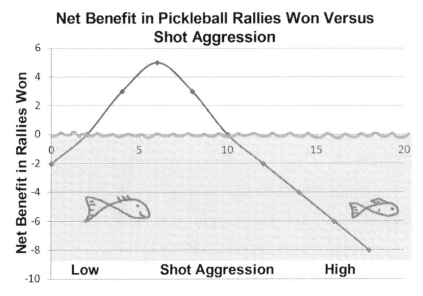

Figure 4-7 Net benefit in pickleball rallies won versus shot aggression

and the location of the optimal level of aggression depend on the shot, and the capability levels of the shot maker and the defender. In situations where the benefits of aggression disappear (such as when serving to advanced players), it makes no sense to incur the penalties that come from high aggression.

Serving Strategy Conclusions/Recommendations

In the social/recreational arena, super serves can often produce many more winners than losers. In this arena, I can't advise against the use of fast serves and trick serves. However, in advanced play, it's very difficult for super serves to be beneficial. Usually it's the opposite.

For folks who are developing their skill my advice is this: focus on reliability. Your game will not be handicapped if you can consistently hit serves that land near the center of the box. Again, even at the very highest skill levels of pickleball, all that is necessary is a serve that does not fault and that can get about halfway back in the box. So, for developing players, I recommend aiming for the middle of the box and allowing at least several feet of clearance above the net.

Many pickleball teachers advise their students to practice serving deep or to backhands. My concern with this is that most attempts to hit targets away from the center of the box result in increased faults. In my opinion, of all the areas to work on in pickleball, working on getting a serve to land deeper than the center of the box should be low on the list.

Common Mistakes

No focus, visualization, or routine. Many social players fault on their serve due to lack of focus and lack of visualizing the target and trajectory. Don't serve while talking and don't serve before spotting your exact target. Again, watch the pro tennis players. They are consistent in their serving routine.

Pickleball Commandment Number 1: Never Miss a Serve

Who knows how many rallies you could have won had you not missed your serve. Per Coach Mo: "If you miss your serve, the only thing your opponent needs to win the rally is a pulse." Most misses come from lack of focus and discipline. So, develop your routine, spot your exact target, ensure your alignment, and push the ball along the trajectory path.

Making it Happen

1. The next time you go out to play, before each serve, spot the target (dead center of the box), and try to hit this target. Keep some mental notes on how well you did. I think you will find that hitting a target is more difficult than you think it is.
2. On your next outing, set a goal to have zero service faults. Count any faults that occur. Coach Mo drives the philosophy that you should not fault with your serve more than once per month.
3. Over your next several outings, develop your serving routine. It should always involve spotting the target and visualizing the ball flight, which should allow a generous clearance of the net and a wide margin for error.

CHAPTER 5: STROKE BASICS

The Fly Swatter, the Merry-Go-Round, & How NOT to Hit the Ball

Most of the instruction in this section is aimed at helping players who have no prior experience in a racquet or paddle sport. As a result, their flailing and swatting actions lead to endless frustration. This chapter should help such folks dramatically improve their ball placement skills.

We will cover all strokes in detail later in this book, but first I'm going to talk about how not to hit the ball. The technique of using a fly swatter is exactly how *not* to hit the ball. When you use a fly swatter, the stroke action comes from the elbow and a quick snap of the wrist. The goal is to generate as much speed as possible and to complete the action very quickly. Many folks who have no prior racquet or paddle skills begin playing pickleball using the fly swatter hitting style. In particular I very often see a stroke I call the sidearm fly swatter. See Figure 5–1. Coach Mo calls this around-the-body swing the Merry-Go-Round swing. He suggests the Ferris wheel as a better carnival ride model for your stroke.

Considering the very rapid curving action of the fly swatter stroke, it would be a miracle if a shot from such a stroke could ever hit a target. The problem with a rapidly curving paddle face is that you must have perfect, split-second timing in order for the ball to go where you want it to go.

Figure 5-1 The Merry-Go-Round swing

What to Do Instead: The One Unit Arm, Hitting "Four Balls in a Row"

In pickleball, the correct stroke seeks to minimize rapid curvature and better ensure that the paddle stays square to the target before, during, and after the strike. For most shots in pickleball, the correct paddle path is linear and forward toward the target. In other words, the paddle is pushed forward along the desired ball flight path. See Figure 5–2. With this technique, the swing does not curve around or wrap around the body.

To achieve this rather linear paddle path, the correct stroke uses essentially no wrist or elbow. Instead, the stroke comes mostly from forward momentum from the weight shift forward and from upper torso turning. Some stroke motion comes from the shoulder. So, among great players in pickleball, the arm operates as "one unit," with essentially no elbow or wrist action.

Figure 5-2 The correct paddle path is linear through the strike

33

Why is the "one unit arm" technique better? In brief, it provides both better ball path accuracy and better distance control. For every pickleball shot I can think of, placement accuracy and precision are much more important than achieving maximum impact velocity. In pickleball, just like when putting or chipping a golf ball, any wrist snapping destroys placement precision and distance control.

Most pickleball coaches advise using a swing style that minimizes rapid curvature such as would come from swatting at the ball. A good stroke approximates a "blocking" or linear action, especially through the strike zone. The "Coach Mo" stroke involves first aiming the paddle, that is, setting the paddle face to point to the desired ball flight path. Thus the paddle face must have the correct direction and lift angle to ensure the ball goes over the net. Next, the stroke attempts to use a rather linear, not curving, paddle path through the strike. See Figure 5–3. Coach Mo often says, "Set the paddle motionless facing the target trajectory, and then pretend you are hitting four balls in a row." To hit four balls in a row requires taking the paddle along a near-linear path for quite a distance. Obviously, any wrist or swatting action would not allow such a linear stroke.

Hit "Four Balls in a Row"

Figure 5-3 The "Coach Mo" stroke

Eliminate the Loop

Tennis strokes such as the topspin forehand ground stroke often use a swing pattern that looks like a loop. Many tennis players bring this big loop swing with them to pickleball. In pickleball, usually the need is for placement precision. Placement precision is better achieved from a compact, aim-and-then-hit-four-balls-in-a-row stroke than from a looping, flailing, or swatting action. A way to think about this is A: ready, B: aim,

C: push. The paddle goes from ready position (A), directly to the aim point and paused motionless (B), and then it is pushed forward through "four balls in a row" (C). See Figure 5-4. Note two important things: 1) the paddle does not "loop" to the aim point but instead goes almost directly there, and 2) there is a moment when the paddle is motionless before it is pushed forward.

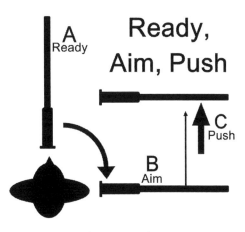

Figure 5-4 Ready, aim, push

From inside the baseline, the ready position would normally have the paddle parallel to the net and you would normally use an open stance (feet parallel to your opponent). In such a case, the ready, aim, contact, follow through sequence would look something like Figure 5-5.

Figure 5-5 Proper strike sequence

Keep the Paddle Level With or Above the Wrist

When making the linear stroke, meet the ball low so that you can get beneath it, preventing the paddle tip from dipping. Your paddle should be level with or above the wrist through the stroke. The importance of this is discussed later in this chapter.

A Story from Joe: Coach Mo's Pointer Paddle Teaching Aid

In preparing for this book, I traveled to The Villages, Florida, to visit Coach Mo. While I was there he showed me a favorite teaching tool he used. It is a "pointer paddle" that has a retractable antenna sticking out of the paddle face. The antenna is at a 90-degree angle or right angle to the paddle face plane. See Figure 5-6. He extended the antenna, handed it to me, and then wisely stepped back a few feet. I could see why he backed up. As I started swinging this thing, the antenna was flying every which way.

He explained to me that the antenna points to the approximate direction the ball will travel after the hit. When holding this special paddle, you quickly discover that any slight wrist movement creates huge directional changes. Likewise, when hold-

Figure 5-6 Coach Mo's pointer paddle

ing this teaching device, it becomes obvious that it's nearly impossible to achieve directional precision when using any type of swatting or curving stroke. Conversely, when holding this special paddle, it becomes apparent that setting the paddle face to the target and then moving it linearly in the direction of the pointer through the strike makes the most sense for achieving shot accuracy. Such a linear paddle movement is called a pushing or blocking stroke as opposed to a curving, swinging stroke.

At my age, there aren't too many things that make me say, "Wow," but this was one of them. This was a powerful teaching aid that clearly showed the problems with rapid swing curvature and the advantages of using a more linear paddle path.

Coach Mo tells students to set the paddle face motionless (have the antenna point to the ball flight path) and then push forward, pretending to hit four balls in a row. See Figure 5-7. You may be asking yourself, "How can I set the paddle face motionless without causing a hiccup in my swing?" When the paddle comes back into the aimed position, it stops for a moment before coming forward whether you want it to or not. You can't change the

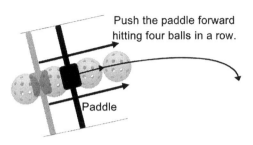

Figure 5-7 Push the paddle forward through "four balls in a row"

paddle direction from back to forward without a moment of zero velocity. It's at this naturally occurring moment that you need to ensure that the paddle face is aimed properly before it moves forward.

As will be discussed later, the ball does not always exit the paddle at a perfect right angle to the paddle face due to spin and other factors. So the pointer is nearly correct but not always exactly correct.

Distance Control

Along with the accuracy benefit, another key benefit of the "one unit arm" is distance control. As discussed in the introduction, the key need for most shots in pickleball is distance control. Just like in golf, if the hands start working independently of the arms, another speed variable is introduced and distance control suffers. Suppose you were trying to use an underhand ball toss to toss a pickleball into a bucket located ten feet in front of you. Likely you would use a stroke resembling the way you would release a bowling ball. Such a stroke would not involve snapping the wrist or bending the elbow. In other words, you would use the one unit arm with the motion coming from torso rotation and the shoulder.

A Fundamental Error: You do not have the control you think you do.

Even great tennis players and great racquetball players have to make adjustments when taking up pickleball. In particular, they find that the ball seems to have a mind of its own. It does not go where you expect it to go. Shots that you think should be good go into the net or out of bounds. At least ten times per game I see the perplexed expression that says, "How did that happen?"

The main reason why ball control is so difficult in pickleball is that neither the ball nor the paddle compresses or "gives." In tennis and in racquetball, the ball compresses or flattens out against the racquet strings and the strings flex to slightly surround the ball. Both of these deflections act to help the ball exit the racquet perpendicular to the racquet face even if the incoming ball is not traveling perpendicular to the racquet face. Racquet strings also "grab the ball" and mostly kill any incoming ball spin rather than allowing it to be passed on to the next person hitting the ball. In pickleball, a heavily applied spin can sometimes be passed along through several hits.

In the case of a pickleball paddle hitting a pickleball, the lack of compression and the passing on of spin degrade ball control. Even the very best players find that they must leave a large margin for error when selecting where to place shots. A beginner mistake is to try to aim shots to land near sidelines. Even advanced players need to imagine the opponent court being smaller than it is.

In addition, you must account for vertical (net clearance) error. Even when dinking very close to the net, the pros usually clear the net by a foot. Think of your first opponent as the net. I often repeat the phrase, "anything but the net." When the ball goes into the net, nobody can save you. Don't let the net beat you; make your opponent beat you. Keep the ball alive and give your opponent a chance to fault.

It might be helpful to remember the "margin for error" model shown in Figure 5-8.

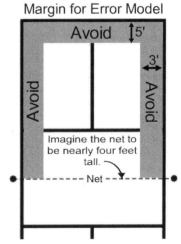

Figure 5-8 Margin for error model

How I Know the Linear Stroke Works

I have a practice wall in my garage. My kids and their friends often see me practicing and sometimes ask if they can try it. So, I hand over my paddle and ball. Of course, when a newcomer tries to do this, the ball goes everywhere and it's rare that more than a few hits in a row can be made before we are chasing the ball. I then explain how to keep the ball going: you simply keep the face of the paddle going back and forth in a line pointed at the target. As soon as you get the paddle speed set in the right rhythm, you can hit the target all day long. See Figure 5-9.

Figure 5-9 If you simplify your stroke so that you keep the paddle pointed at the target while going straight forward and back, you can dink to a wall target all day long

A Footnote

I am sure that many players and coaches will take issue with the notion of setting the paddle face and then making a linear strike through the contact point. Many will nitpick this and point out that such a "set-then-push" stroke is essentially impossible and not used by the pros. Indeed, I agree. Swing paths always have some fluidity and curvature no matter how much you may try to keep a linear path through "four balls in a row."

Although the pickleball stroke is more compact than the tennis stroke, which involves a longer backswing and follow through than the pickleball stroke, the aiming and linear hitting advice is the same for pickleball as tennis. The United States Tennis Association (USTA) book *Coaching Tennis Successfully* advises, "Ball direction is controlled by the racket face at impact . . . [the goal is] elongating the contact point . . . players must push the racket through the entire contact area . . . the follow through should extend toward the target."

Top coaches, both in tennis and in pickleball, agree on all of the following:
- The "one unit arm" concept is correct and the wristy fly swatter technique is bad.
- The paddle or racquet has to be "in the slot" and traveling on the correct line ahead of contact with the ball. You must ultimately square the face to the ball and target line to achieve placement accuracy.
- A good mental image is to elongate the contact zone, pushing the paddle or racket through the contact zone, pretending to hit four balls in a row.
- Follow through should extend toward the target.

When you watch very slow motion videos of the strokes used by the pro-level players you definitely see all of the above characteristics.

Good ball placement capability and error reduction are what pickleball players at all levels need. How do we get there? We get there by reducing rapidly curving and swatting motions and better controlling the paddle face direction and speed before impact and through impact.

Paddle Holding Basics & Keeping the Tip Up

Whenever you watch the pro tennis players make volleys at the net, low volleys, half volleys, or really low ground strokes, you may notice that

Figure 5-10 Raquet angle in tennis

they always maintain an angle of at least 45 degrees between the racquet and their forearm. Often the angle is fully 90 degrees such that the racquet and the forearm are perpendicular. See Figure 5-10. This results from perhaps a century or more of rigid training and coaching. The advice is to always keep the racquet tip up, with the racquet head above the wrist. The coach ingrains that you must see wrinkles at the wrist joint. See Figure 5-11.

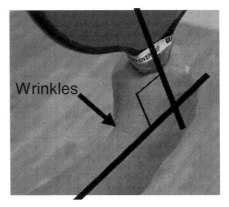

Figure 5-11 Wrinkles on the wrist

Indeed, all of the above advice is sound and such form is seen in all of the top players. In pickleball also, the best players use these same keep-the-tip-up/keep-the-wrist-angle-intact techniques. But why is this the best way? What's the benefit? Why can't the racquet tip go low? Why can't we use the racquet like a shovel or scoop? Why can't the handle of the paddle be in line with the forearm?

Here's the rationale for keeping the tip up and keeping the wrist angle intact.

The Strongest Hold and Grip is at 90 Degrees

Your grip strength is maximized when the handle is perpendicular to the forearm and strength is reduced as the angle is diminished. Suppose you need a good, strong grip on a hammer or hatchet. You would hold it with the handle perpendicular to the forearm. Suppose you are using a grip strengthening exerciser. You would hold it as shown in Figure 5-12.

Figure 5-12 Maximum grip strength

41

Better Mis-Hit Results, Fewer Shots Dumped into the Net

When a fast-moving pickleball impacts a paddle, the paddle can deflect, especially if the ball hits near the tip or near an edge. If the paddle tip is already low, an impact deflection of the tip will almost certainly send the ball low and into the net. However, if the paddle tip is held above the wrist, an impact deflection of the tip will send the ball higher, better ensuring it will go over the net.

Paddle Head Lag from Rapid Acceleration

Here's another problem that happens when the paddle tip is low. Acceleration, and especially sudden acceleration, causes the paddle tip to fall back or lag. When this happens with an underhand shot, the paddle can often be pointing downward at the moment of impact, sending the ball into the net. This happens often when a novice tries to make a fast forehand drive. If the tip is up instead, any unwanted lag causes the ball to go higher, not lower. See Figure 5-13.

Figure 5-13 Disadvantage of holding the paddle tip low

Allows Imparting Backspin

If the tip of the paddle is pointed low, as would be used for a scooping or shoveling type of stroke, it's nearly impossible to add any backspin to the ball. You may not use spin, but the best players need this option. The most often used spin is backspin and this is usually applied with the paddle being parallel to the ground and held in a hammer-like grip. See Figure 5-14.

Adding Spin

Figure 5-14 Adding spin

Easier Transition between Low and High Play

If the tip of the paddle is pointed low, as would be used for a scooping or shoveling type of stroke, what do you do if the ball comes high to your forehand, above your "scoop?" You would need to bend your elbow and scrunch up the scoop to a location, say, near your hip. At this point, the face of the paddle is almost certainly pointing severely upwards. Notice that from this "high scoop" position, it's nearly impossible to angle the paddle face to a level or downward position. If the ball arrives any higher, then you are jammed. See Figure 5-15.

Now let's say you are playing all shots, even low dink shots, with the tip slightly up. If the ball suddenly comes high, when you raise your paddle you should be able to avoid getting jammed. In pickleball, you might be very low and involved in a dinking exchange and then, in just a fraction of a second, you are involved in a volley war. Pickleball coaches and tennis coaches agree that when volleying, to the extent possible, you need to follow the tip up/elbow low/90-degree wrist angle technique. If you are already using the 90-degree wrist angle when dinking, you can transition quickly to volleying with good technique.

With the tip down scoop, you get "jammed" if the ball comes high.

With the tip up method, it's easier to go from low to high.

Figure 5-15 The tip up method provides an easier transition between low and high play

Easier to Cover a Wide Range

Now let's say you are using the paddle tip low/scooping technique and the ball unexpectedly comes wide to your forehand. Now the scoop goes out to the side, the swing involves curvature, and ball control degrades. The "tip up" method allows better handling of shots that are low, high, and out to the side. Note that the tip up style of play requires that you lower your body so that your hand is below the paddle center rather than above it. It's more work, but it's better to lower and compress to allow keeping the paddle tip up than to stand tall and allow the paddle to drop to parallel, or worse, to allow the paddle tip to dip.

Figure 5-16 Tip up versus tip down

Easier to Control the Paddle Face Angle

A key need in pickleball is to be able to control the paddle face angle before and completely through impact, making a linear or near linear path through the strike. The "tip low" scoop technique essentially requires paddle swing path curvature. When the tip is low, getting the upward angle you need means you must have perfect timing. With the tip up method, you are already compressed and beneath the ball. This should better permit making a linear push forward through the strike. Tennis pros say that you have better vertical angle control of the head when the head is above your wrist than when the head is below your wrist. See Figure 5-17.

Keeps Your Paddle near Your Center

The more you extend your arm and reach away from your body to hit, the more you lose control and accuracy. Whenever your opponent can

Tip Up Versus Tip Down
Paddle Face Control

The tip down method creates stroke curvature

The tip up method allows a push forward linear strike

It's easier to control the angle with the tip above your hand

Figure 5-17 Tip up versus tip down paddle face control

force you to make a wide reach-out, he has almost certainly caused you to make a bad shot. Scooping and shoveling paddle strokes are usually made in a rather lazy way, with the knees rather straight and with the arm extended and reaching. The "tip up" paddle strokes are made with the knees bent and with the paddle closer to your center. Your strongest and most reliable shots will happen when you are reaching less.

Comments and Recommendations

As both authors of this book come from a tennis background and use mostly tennis techniques for playing pickleball, we are advocates of the very long established tennis techniques, including those discussed above. There are a few tennis techniques (like looping strokes and long backswings) that should not be used in pickleball and we discuss these where appropriate.

Should you change your style if you are using scoop-from-beneath techniques? Should you change if you are using ground stroke techniques that resemble serving techniques (scooping from beneath)? If this were tennis, a tennis professional would emphatically say yes, but pickleball is not tennis. Many pickleball competitors use scoop/shovel dinking techniques with good results. The key is achieving consistency and being able to field and place shots reliably. If you do choose to scoop, you need to try to keep the stroke very linear through the strike zone. Stepping into the shot and having forward momentum through the strike can help make a scooping stroke more linear. The underhand serve motion can work well for the third shot drop (described later), but, again, the motion through the strike zone needs to be linear. Again, achieving consistency is the key.

Figure 5-18 Tip up versus tip down

I urge all scoop-from-beneath players to at least try playing with the paddle staying at or above parallel (to the ground) and with the wrinkles in the wrist (i.e., with the paddle handle being at 45–90 degrees to the forearm). I think many players will find that going from tip down to tip up will transform their game.

Making it Happen

1. If you have access to a practice wall, practice by thinking Ready, Aim, Push. Try to eliminate long, looping, or rapidly curving swing paths and replace them with compact, more linear (pushing) paths.

2. On your next outing, think Ready, Aim, Push when making your shots.

3. On a future outing or when using a practice wall, try to get beneath the ball, keeping the paddle level with the ground or with the tip up.

CHAPTER 6: FOOTWORK SKILLS AND MOVEMENT BASICS

Throughout the book, I discuss where to position yourself and when, where, and how to move. This short chapter introduces some general basics of pickleball movement. Doubles pickleball position locations, movement directions, and the footwork patterns to get there are rather simple. The basic objective is to move your team fully forward as quickly as possible and then have your team stay fully forward and linked together. Once fully forward, your team moves laterally as necessary, staying linked, using shuffle steps. Usually, only a lob and perhaps an imminent smash should bring your team off the NVZ line.

Here are some basics.

Avoid Traveling Backwards

You should not travel backwards unless you must, and there are only a few legitimate circumstances that require traveling backwards. Most retreats stem from positioning and readiness errors. Here's what I see happen all the time in social/recreational play: players fail to get fully forward and instead position themselves in the middle of the service box. So, their feet are fully exposed to their opponents. In addition, these players are not compressed in a good, ready position that allows fielding shots coming low or toward their feet. So, when a shot comes anywhere near their feet, they attempt to scramble backwards. If they successfully return the shot, they only come forward to the same place where they were before. Thus the forward and back cycle can repeat. I've seen many falls result from the awkward forward and back retreat cycles.

To avoid backward travel remember these rules:

1. When on the serving team, stay behind the baseline with the server until the return of serve shot can be judged. A mistake is to move forward too early. If you move in too early or too far and the shot comes in deep, you have no choice but to retreat as the "double bounce rule" prohibits hitting a volley. As you will learn later, it's tough making a good third shot. It's even more difficult trying to make a good third shot while retreating.

2. When on the return of serve team, the service returner should stay behind the baseline in the ready position until the serve can be judged. His or her partner should be fully forward at the NVZ line before the serve is made. Fully forward means the toes are no more than two inches away from the line. Once the return of serve is made, the service returner should quickly run forward and be fully forward at the NVZ line before the next shot—the third shot—comes across the net. About the only shots that should cause either of these players to back up or move away from the line are lob shots or imminent smashes. These at-the-line players must stay compressed in a basketball-like ready position to allow the fielding of shots coming toward their feet, to allow hitting low volleys, and to allow quick shuffle stepping or scrambling as necessary to reach shots.

3. When on the serving team and attempting to make the critical third shot drop shot into the kitchen, transfer your weight forward during the hit, quickly assess the quality of your shot, and, if it's good (not attackable), you and your partner need to scramble forward making as much forward progress as possible, hopefully getting established at the NVZ line. If you can't get fully forward

before your opponent hits the ball, stop, split step, and get compressed at the moment your opponent touches the ball. Unless a great opportunity presents, continue the drop shot and scramble sequence until you can get your team fully forward. A common mistake is to hit a great third shot but not fully utilize the opportunity to quickly move forward. Top players can usually get fully forward to the NVZ line if they make a good third shot drop.

4. Whenever you are stopped in "no man's land," you need to be compressed and lowered so that you can hit low volleys or half volleys rather than having to back up. This is a key skill to practice and you can use a practice wall to do it. Here's how. Get compressed and lowered and hit shots at the wall that will rebound toward your feet. If you can volley it back, do so. Otherwise hit a half volley (i.e., a shot that is hit immediately after the ball bounces, well before it reaches the apex of its bounce).

5. Once all players are fully forward at the NVZ line, most movements will be lateral (sideways like a crab) only, with the desired style being a side shuffle step. Any shot coming toward your feet should be volleyed back rather than allowing a bounce. The top players stay tightly pinned to the line during typical dinking and volley exchanges.

Notice that the footwork, especially for the service return team, is really easy. One member of this team should already have both toes pinned to the NVZ line. All the service return player has to do is return the serve, with a semi-lob if necessary, and run forward to get both feet pinned to the line before the third shot comes across the net. From this point, mostly side shuffles during the dinking game are required.

Lateral Movements

In pickleball, lateral movements follow the same rules as in tennis. To the extent possible, you should try to protect your ready position "base" (i.e., protect your ready position, feet-apart stance). So, if you only need to go a short distance, take a step to the side and then get back to the ready

position. If you need
to move more, use
a side shuffle step.
This keeps you fac-
ing your opponent
and best allows you
to change directions
quickly if necessary.
Avoid closing your
feet fully together
on this shuffle step.
Instead, try to
maintain as much
base width as possi-
ble while shuffling.
Although shuffling

Figure 6-1 Basic steps

is preferable, when dinking you can make a crossover step, say, to reach
to a sideline, and still recover to a ready position as long as your shot is a
soft (unattackable) dink into the kitchen.

If you must travel further and faster, you may have to turn and use a
crossing or running step. If you have to go really far, really quick, you will
have to turn and run. In any case, you need to try to get set, if possible,
to execute your shot. Sometimes, of course, you will be forced to hit on
the run.

Forward Movements

If you only need to go a short distance forward, use a forward shuffle
(gallop) step. You might use such a step when making a slight adjustment forward when receiving a serve. If you need to get somewhere fast,
like getting to the net after returning a serve or getting forward following
a third shot, run, but stop and split step if your opponent hits the ball
before you get fully forward.

Backward Movements

Let's look at some common scenarios where you need to retreat.

1. *Deep, small adjustment.* Suppose you are just behind the baseline but the return of serve is coming really deep and fast. In such a case where a small movement is required, turn sideways to the ball (like a batter) and use a sideways shuffle to set up for the ground stroke.

2. *Short, disguised offensive lob from the NVZ line.* From this close range, a disguised, good lob will be past you in less than a second. Usually, all you can do is drop one foot back and then leap. If your reflexes are too slow for this, you will need to turn and run and hit the lob after it bounces.

3. *A high, deep, defensive lob, but sure to be in bounds.* Here is a case where you have time to set up. Turn sideways to the ball and do a side shuffle or side-cross-side step sequence to get behind the ball. This is the way a quarterback in football turns and "drops back."

4. *A deep lob that might go out of bounds.* Let's say you are at the net and you get surprised by a deep lob. Your partner yells "bounce it," as it might go out of bounds. In such a case, will need to turn, run, and set up to play the bounced ball if it bounces in bounds.

5. *Backing out of the kitchen.* Many players avoid ever stepping into the kitchen. So long as the ball bounces, a step into the kitchen could allow you to make a better shot. However, when you do step in, do so with one foot only and then push off of this foot to re-establish yourself outside of the kitchen.

6. *An imminent close-range smash.* Let's say you or your partner just made a terrible offensive lob from the NVZ line, giving your fully forward opponent an easy overhead smash shot. You've got a big problem and there's no good solution. Fit and fast players may be able to get back a few steps and hope to make a block. If there's no time to move, get your paddle set to block and hope for a miracle.

Staying Linked to Your Partner

Beginner pickleball players usually seek to defend their side of the court only. The thinking is "this is my side and that is your side. I'll look after my side and you look after your side." Going along with this is the feeling that, "I can't give up defending my side to move over and help you. If I do, I risk having a shot come back to my side that I can't cover." Such a defense gets picked apart quickly by good players who will angle a shot to draw an opponent to the side and then hit the next shot down the middle.

The Defensive Wall Slides in Relation to the Position of the Ball

The Partners Must Stay Linked Together

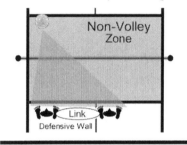

Advanced players don't think like this at all. Instead, they are passionate about helping out whoever is closest to the ball by ensuring that the opponent cannot make a "down-the-middle" shot. In order to protect against the deadly down-the-middle shot, smart teammates stay tightly linked together, moving forward and back together and moving side to side together. The two teammates seek to form a wall that is parallel to the net and that moves in relation to the position of the ball. Communications like "go," "come up," and "get back" are helpful.

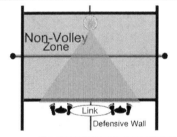

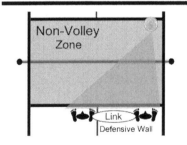

Figure 6-2 The defensive wall of linked players

When the ball is near your teammate's sideline, he will need to cover the line and you will need to slide over to prevent the down-the-middle shot. Likewise, when the ball is near your sideline, you will need to cover the line and your partner will need to slide over to prevent the down-the-middle shot. When the down-the-middle shot is successful, the coverage fault is usually not from the person covering the line, but from his or her partner.

When tightly linked together forming a wall, the teammates will indeed leave part of the court uncovered. When dinking or whenever the ball is moving slow, this is not a problem because the wall can slide with enough time to cover sideline-to-sideline shots. However, if your opponent receives a volley opportunity, he might be able to send a shot crosscourt to the open area that outraces the wall. Still, the highest percentage action is to protect against the down-the-middle shot even if it means a distant area will not be covered. See Figure 6-2. When fully forward, both teammates need to watch out for the down-the-middle shot, which might be cleverly disguised, thus taking away some of your time to react. Likewise, if you see the opponent wall break open, keep your cool, disguise your intent, and send a shot down the middle.

Many beginners think they can simply take a step to cover the down-the-middle hole. You do not have time to take a step. When playing forward, even the very fastest 5.0-rated players cannot take a step to cover the hole. Wherever you are standing when your opponent hits the down-the-middle shot is where you will be standing when it has gone past you. So, stay linked tightly enough to your partner that your paddles could overlap. See Figure 6-3.

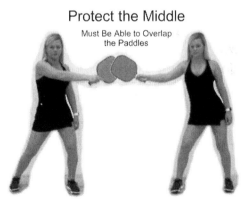

Protect the Middle

Must Be Able to Overlap the Paddles

Figure 6-3 Protect the middle

Making it Happen

1. On your next outing, make mental notes of your backwards movements. Ask yourself if they would have been necessary if you had been compressed and ready and positioned correctly to start with.

2. On your next outing, make some notes about shots that successfully came down the middle. Were you ready? Were you in place?

CHAPTER 7: COMMON COURT TERMS AND TARGETS

The diagrams below show features and areas of the pickleball court. You may need to refer to these often. You should become famil-

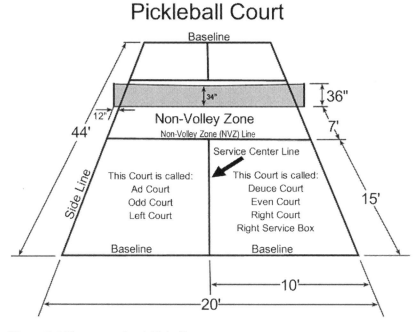

Figure 7-1 The parts of a pickleball court

iar with all of the terms shown such as the Non-Volley Zone, Non-Volley Zone Line, No Man's Land, baseline, side line, deuce court, even court, etc.

The Left Heel Target

Perhaps the most important target on the court in pickleball is the "Left Heel Target." Even though I call it the left heel target, the left heel target of the left opponent is about mid-way between your opponents but slightly closer to the left opponent, causing a very difficult low-to-the-backhand return shot (for a right-handed player). Notice also that the "left heel target" is not "heel deep" when the opponent is very deep in the court or behind the baseline. Why?

The target must allow a margin for error and prevent the mistake of going out of bounds. Figure 7-3 shows the location of the left heel target in various situations.

Most errors and "flubs" occur when players are hitting backhand shots. The most difficult such shot is low and requires a "reach out." A second advantage of going to the left heel target is that a ball hit from this location essentially prohibits your opponent from making a strong or aggressive shot.

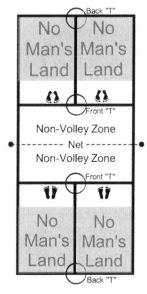

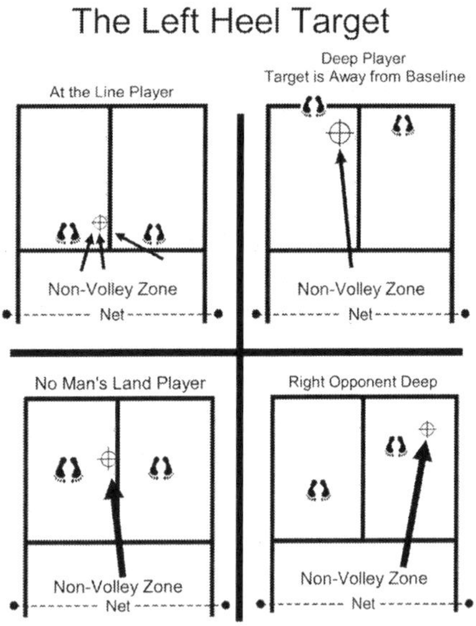

Figure 7-2 The Ts and no man's land areas

The Left Heel Target

Figure 7-3 The left heel target

If you get confused or can't remember the left heel target, aim to place the ball so that it will bounce on the court right in the middle between where the left opponent is standing and the right opponent is standing. Of course you must avoid aiming for a target too close to the baseline.

The Low to the Backhand Left Heel Target

Figure 7-4 The low to the backhand left heel target

Making it Happen

On your next several outings, focus on hitting most of your shots to the left heel target and avoid giving your opponent volley shots. Seek to make the ball bounce near the left heel target. With some practice on this, you can get to a point where you no longer have to think about the left heel target. Instead, you hit to this difficult to reach location automatically.

CHAPTER 8: READY POSITION AND THE SPLIT STEP

In this chapter, I discuss some basic elements of all back court ground strokes, whether forehand or backhand. A ground stroke means you are hitting the ball after it has bounced on the ground. Back court means in the back half of the court toward the baseline, not near the NVZ line. These back court shots include the return of serve shot and the return of the return of serve shot, i.e., the third shot. Ground strokes at the NVZ are usually "dink" shots, which will be discussed later.

In singles tennis, almost all shots are back court ground strokes. The players usually hit from baseline to baseline. These ground stroke shots are hard and fast and they are intended to "out race" the person trying to return them. In doubles pickleball, the situation is opposite. Very few shots are back court ground strokes—usually only the return of serve and the third shot. In addition, neither of these shots needs to be fast. In fact, the best third shot is usually a soft drop shot designed to land in the kitchen area. So, strategically played doubles pickleball contains very few ground strokes that are played from the back court area.

Behind the Baseline Ready Position

Now let's get back to talking about technique. Whether you are waiting for the serve or waiting for the return of the serve, you need to be in a proper "ready position" to allow you to quickly move to the ball. The goal of your movement is to create the ideal set up so that you can hit the ball at the perfect location in your stance and at the perfect location in your swing path. It's just like in golf: a consistent set up leads to a consistent shot. Likewise, poor shots usually come from reaching to hit the ball or from trying to hit while running.

In making improvements in your pickleball game, some skills are really easy to learn and implement and others are very difficult. Making a commitment to always be in the ready position for receiving the serve and for receiving the return of serve should be a "no-brainer," as the "bang for the buck" is so great.

You might be thinking, with the court so small and with a wiffle ball moving so slowly compared to a tennis ball, is it really necessary to get into the tennis-like ready position? I will answer this below.

Aside from playing pickleball, one of my hobbies is making video recordings of pickleball games. I record and collect hundreds of hours of games, some at the recreational level, and some at the high skill level. I load these video files onto my computer and then watch each rally in slow motion to detect the root cause of the loss of the rally.

Among advanced players, service "aces" are very rare and faults on the return of serve are rare. (A service ace refers to a serve that never gets touched even though it was in bounds or "good.") However, in recreational play, service aces are not uncommon and return-of-serve faults are very common. So what is the root cause of service aces among recreational players? In most cases, I find that the receiver was standing straight up and flat footed, unable to move quickly. In other words, the service receiver was essentially unready. Indeed, when you are standing tall, with your feet close together, and with your weight evenly distributed between heels and toes, you are "glued" in place, unable to move in any direction very quickly. In order to move, you must first lower and bend your knees. It's nearly impossible to jump from a stiff-legged standing position. Likewise, it's difficult to move quickly in any direction from a standing-straight-up position.

To really bring home the point, try this test. While standing straight up and flat-footed, try to move quickly to the left and then to the right using a shuffling type of footwork. Now try it starting from a compressed, basketball-like ready position with your weight forward on the balls of your feet. I think you will agree that your agility is enormously better when you use the compressed, ready position.

So, to answer the question above—is it really necessary to get into the tennis-like ready position—the answer is yes if you want to start eliminating aces and service return faults.

Let's look at the details of the ready stance. It is the same as in tennis and it's the same as in many other sports. I think it is worthwhile to watch the professional tennis players on YouTube or on the Tennis Channel. Especially pay attention to the position they are in as they are about to receive the serve.

Their feet are not shoulder width apart, but wider, allowing better side-to-side quickness. Their knees are bent and their weight is on the balls of their feet. Their arms and their racket are out in front of their body and both hands are on their racket. They have a forward lean so that they are at least a foot shorter than their normal height. This creates a lower center of gravity, which facilitates rapid movement. When you are compressed in such a manner, you can move in any direction quickly and you can better field shots that are aimed at your feet.

Behind the Baseline
Ready Position

Figure 8-1 Behind the baseline ready position

So, to recap: set your feet rather wide apart, bend your knees, lean forward to get low, and stay on the balls of your feet. Keep your paddle up and out in front of you with both hands on it. The paddle should be cocked up so that the paddle face is above your wrists. The paddle blade should be perpendicular to the net. Notice that the tip of the middle finger of the non-dominant hand rests at the center of the paddle "sweet spot." To add extra agility, use the split step described below.

Split Step

Another thing to notice as you watch the professionals play tennis is a movement called the split step. Using YouTube or the Tennis Channel, watch the service receiver waiting in the ready position. At about the moment the server makes contact with the ball, the receiver makes a slight jump and lands again in the compressed, ready position. This creates a dynamic ready position, instead of a static one. When timed perfectly, the player lands, compresses, and rebounds into the needed direction in a fast, continuous, and fluid manner. This action is a compress/release, or rebound, which allows explosive movement. The key for the split step is timing.

When Receiving a Serve

In professional tennis, service receivers perform this action without fail, as so much depends on it. The serve is the most important shot in tennis, as the serve accounts for about one third of all points a player earns. The serve is traveling at more than 100 miles per hour and the receiver has to cover a width of about 15 feet at the location where he is standing. In fact, even the very best of tennis players cannot cover the full width. Instead, they get aced when the ball lands near the service box sides. The service receiver not only has to get to the ball, but get to it quickly to allow the best setup possible.

How about in pickleball? Pickleball is much more forgiving. Even a very fast pickleball serve is only about 40 miles per hour, and most serves are only about 20 miles per hour. In addition, the receiver needs to cover a smaller width of the court. So, do you need to do this split step action when receiving the serve in pickleball? Certainly it's a best practice. If you are sometimes aced by short serves or serves to the edges, the split step would help. It will also help you avoid the situations where you barely get to a serve, thereby making return faults or weak returns.

When you watch the top 5.0-rated professional pickleball players, you will see that many perform the split step when receiving a serve, but most do not. The pickleball serve is more forgiving than the tennis serve and most 5.0-rated players can reach and return any serve from a static ready position.

When Stopped in No Man's Land

There is a common situation where all top players use the split step: when they are making forward progress toward the NVZ line, but then their opponent at the net hits the ball back. Here's an example. Your opponents have returned the serve and now they are fully forward. You are attempting to get forward, so you attempt to hit a drop shot into the kitchen (i.e., you are attempting to execute the soft "third shot drop"). You hit the ball, it looks like it will bounce in the kitchen, and you immediately start scrambling forward. Unfortunately, your shot could be reached before it bounced, so your opponent has volleyed it back, and you are still six feet behind the NVZ line. In other words, you are trapped in "no man's land" with a shot probably coming toward your feet or to an open space to your side. In such a case, you need the maximum agility possible. The best thing to do in this situation is to stop and get into split step at the moment your opponent touches the ball. This will allow you to move sideways or to field a low shot directed at your feet. If, instead of stopping, you continue running forward, you will not be able to field low shots or shots that require a step to either side. So, never sacrifice being in a good ready position for a better position on the court. If you are not stopped and properly prepared to hit the ball, your shot will likely fail even if you are hitting it from a slightly better court position.

Here's a strategy tip. If you are the net man in the above situation and you see

Mid-Court
(No Man's Land)
Ready Position

Figure 8-2 No man's land ready position. You must be lowered, compressed, and ready to field low shots. The paddle should be angled up and in a blocking position.

your opponent running forward, just place the ball so that it will bounce a step or two to either side of the runner. Such shots are nearly impossible for a running person to return.

When Dinking

When engaged in dinking with skilled opponents, you will need a great deal of agility, especially if your opponents can disguise their shots or use "misdirection" shots (shots that appear to be directed one way, but instead go another way). The split step offers the best agility. However many top players do not use the split step during dinking as they are fast enough to field any dink shot from a static ready position. So, many top players use the split step routinely during dinking, but many do not.

Keep in mind that just because your favorite pro does not use the split step when receiving serves or when dinking does not mean that there is no consequence for you to act likewise. In fact, it's the opposite. The slower you are, the more you need to use the split step. Also, less-quick players may need to execute the split step even before their opponent makes contact with the ball.

Figure 8-3 *The value of being compressed in split step*

Common Mistakes

A common mistake when in split step is straightening the knees, rising up, or lifting the head. Instead, you need to stay down and level through the stroke.

Summary & Making it Happen

As I said earlier, in making improvements in your pickleball game, some skills are really easy to learn and implement and others are very difficult. Here are three simple things that anybody can do that will quickly improve their game:

1. Always focus before serving. Spot the target and visualize the trajectory.
2. Always be in the ready position for receiving the serve, for receiving the return of serve, and for receiving every other shot.
3. Get into split step when you get trapped in no man's land.

CHAPTER 9: DEVELOP A WAY TO PRACTICE

Following this chapter, we will discuss stroke techniques, like how to execute forehand and backhand ground strokes, etc. None of this instruction is going to "stick" if it is not practiced and "grooved into" muscle memory. Unfortunately, you can't get much better at pickleball by just playing and doing the same things you have always done. Certain shots in pickleball cannot be learned during regular game play. Here's an example. You are close to the net and suddenly a fastball comes right toward your stomach. All you can do is react. Unless you've practiced and rehearsed a response to such a shot, you will likely miss the ball, mis-hit the ball, or dump it into the net. However, you can practice such fast volley situations with drills until you develop a good volley technique that becomes automatic and reflexive.

No matter what the sport is, the path to greatness involves: 1) getting expert instruction, 2) practice, practice, practice, 3) evaluating results, 4) having the coach define the gaps and needs, and 5) repeating the cycle. In addition to this, serious players have a ball machine, a committed practice partner, and a regular practice schedule.

I realize that most folks do not have the resources or inclination to follow the above path. Rather than having a coach, you may have to use books or videos. Rather than having a ball machine and a practice partner, you may need to use a practice wall.

At a minimum, I think you need a convenient place where you can practice almost every day, irrespective of the weather, or availability of a practice partner. A great resource would be a basement or garage wall. I have a wall in my garage where I can practice. I also have access to my church gymnasium and to my health club gymnasium. There are many, many skills that you can practice using a wall. There are many good YouTube videos that show pickleball wall practice drills.

Along with helping you groove in the stroke techniques described in this book, wall practice helps improve your eye-hand coordination so that you can reduce flubs and mis-hits. Wall practice drills also improve your reaction time.

If you have no other option at your home than the interior dry walls, you can use a Nerf ball of other foam ball for practicing.

Some important drills can only be done with a practice partner. Again, I am lucky to have a practice partner who shares my enthusiasm. Later in this book, I will share some of these drills that require a practice partner.

Just hitting a ball against a wall is not nearly as valuable as designing and executing wall practice challenges. To set up such challenges, you need to set up the wall. If you are using a health club gymnasium wall, use removable painter's tape to set up the imaginary net and wall targets. My garage wall is set up as shown in Figure 9-1. Notice I set the top of the net a little higher than a real net. I do this to try to train myself to always hit higher than the net.

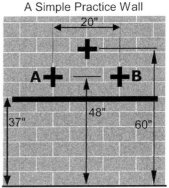

A Simple Practice Wall

Figure 9-1 A simple practice wall

Using the wall setup described and some things we've learned so far, here are some starter drills you can try.

Dinking Directional Control, Alternating Forehand and Backhand Dinks to the Targets

Alternately hit a forehand dink to Target A and then a backhand dink to Target B. Try to do this over and over to the point where you essentially never have a failure. Let the ball bounce between hits. Here is a secret: aim the paddle at the target well in advance and then push it through linearly (pretend to hit several balls in a row) for each shot. I doubt you can become very good at this drill by swatting or swinging the paddle. If the above drill is too difficult, forget about the targets and just try to get forehand and backhand dink shots over the net.

Volleying Directional Control, Alternating Forehand and Backhand Volleys to the Targets

This drill is more difficult than the one above. Alternately hit a forehand volley shot (no bounce) to Target A and then a backhand volley shot to Target B. Or, alternately hit a forehand volley shot to Target A and then a backhand volley shot also to Target A. Try to do this over and over. Try to avoid having the ball ever hit the ground. Use the technique described above: aim the paddle at the target and then push it through linearly (pretend to hit several balls in a row) for each shot. Again, I doubt you can become very good at this drill by swatting or swinging the paddle. See Figure 9-2.

Although the above drills may seem like a challenge at first, with a few weeks of regular practice, I think you will make remarkable progress. The best part is that the improved directional control will improve your game immediately.

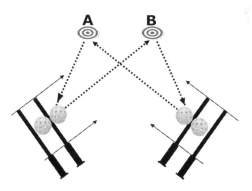

Figure 9-2 Alternating forehand and backhand volley shots against a practice wall

Many folks seem incredulous and skeptical when I suggest wall practice. I'm not sure why. For some reason, most tennis players understand the benefit of wall practice and are advocates of it.

- Says tennis great Novak Djokovic while giving a wall practice demonstration, "The best sparring partner you can have is the wall, guys. Trust me. It never misses."
- Says former World No. 1 tennis great Andre Agassi while giving a practice wall demonstration, "What you can work on out here is not only concentration but racquet head acceleration . . . and even work on your footwork a little bit, which couldn't hurt, like this . . . don't get discouraged when you try this. People who think this is easy really haven't tried it themselves. Look how quickly I have to get in position to hit the ball. It's not easy, especially the concentration factor."
- Says former World No. 1 tennis great Andy Murray, who has a video of himself doing wall practice, "Which opponent has no weakness, never misses and has never lost? The wall."

Making it Happen

1. Find a wall. I do not see how you will groove in the techniques described herein unless you have a readily accessible practice wall or practice partner and facility.
2. Design your wall practice drills and practice every day.

CHAPTER 10: STRATEGY BASICS

A Brief Introduction to the Classic "At the Line Doubles Pickleball Strategy"

If you watch the best pickleball players, you will usually see the following basic strategy unfold. The goal is to get both members of your team fully forward (toes only an inch or two behind the NVZ line) as quickly as possible while also trying to keep your opponents away from the net. So the partner of the service receiver starts with a fully forward position at the NVZ line. Then, as soon as the service receiver returns the serve, he will quickly scramble forward to be alongside his or her partner before the next shot comes back. So, at this point, both members of the service receiving team are fully forward and have the first dominance of the net. At this point, their strategy is to keep the other team (the serving team) from getting forward. Notice that the service receiving team should only need to play one back court ground stroke (the return of serve) before getting fully forward.

The serving team has more of a challenge in getting fully forward. With the double bounce rule, they must wait for the return of serve shot to bounce before they move forward. So, the serving team has a problem: they are facing two opponents who are fully forward, creating a "wall" at the NVZ line. If the serving team hits any rather high shot to the wall, their opponents will smash it back or at least volley it back. If the serving team elects to stay back, they will likely lose the rally because net players have a huge strategic advantage over players who are deep in the court.

In this situation, the classic and most often used approach to get forward is to hit a drop shot or soft shot into the kitchen. Such a slow shot provides some time for the serving team to race forward to the NVZ line, hopefully getting there or almost there before the drop shot can be returned. Notice that the serving team, if successful with the drop shot, may only need to play one back court ground stroke (the third shot drop shot) before getting fully forward. All top players agree that the most important shot in pickleball is the third shot.

If everything goes right for both teams, all players are now fully forward, at the NVZ line. What happens now? With the teams so close together, it's unwise to let the ball get high. Usually a cautious dinking game begins, where each team seeks to feed the other team unattackable dink shots that land in or very near the kitchen. If the ball gets high, a put-away shot occurs. All of the above describes the general way that the professionals play, called "at the line pickleball."

The above is a very concise and by no means comprehensive guide to classic competitive pickleball strategy. For a complete treatment of this subject, please refer to my other book, *At the Line Pickleball: The Winning Doubles Pickleball Strategy*.

To become a good doubles pickleball player, you must understand the vital importance of getting fully forward quickly, you must understand the importance of keeping your opponents away from the net, and you must develop the skills to do both. Your proficiency with these skills will usually determine your overall pickleball skill rating, for example, whether you are a 3.0-rated player or a 5.0-rated player.

Why is Getting Fully Forward Quickly So Important?

As we start talking about the return of serve shot and the third shot (the return of the return of serve) in the next chapters, you will see the extreme emphasis on getting your team fully forward to the NVZ line. Many folks fail to understand and embrace this importance. So, in brief, here's why you must get fully forward quickly:

1. The best offensive and defensive arrangement is when both partners are fully forward and linked together at the NVZ line. It's the best offensive position because you have the widest range of shot angles available, both horizontally (side to side) and vertically (up and down, which allows smashing the ball downward). Fully forward is the best defensive position because the closer you are to your opponent, the better able you are to shield your court from your opponent. Fully forward is the best location to be when you are trying to keep the other team away from the net. This will be discussed more below. Fully forward means that the toes are only one or two inches behind the NVZ line.

2. The closer you are to the net, the easier it is to get the ball over the net. Imagine if you were allowed to stand up against the net. At this location, even the worst flub or mis-hit would go across the net.

3. If, when on the service receiving team, you fail to secure the net immediately, you will likely allow your opponent to take first control of the net.

The Flashlight Beam Model

Imagine for a moment that you have a flashlight and you have an opaque lens cover for the flashlight. Of course, when the lens cover is attached, all light from the flashlight is blocked. Now let's say you remove the lens cap and hold it about a half inch away from the lens. Most of the light would be blocked but some light would escape. Now let's say that you hold the lens cap about five inches away from the lens. At this location, maybe 30 percent of the light is blocked and the rest escapes. Now let's say that you hold the lens cap about three feet away from the lens. At this location, almost no light is blocked.

This is how defending your pickleball court works. The light beam represents your opponent and his or her shot possibilities. The lens cover represents the court defender. The closer you are to the person with the ball, the better you can block his or her shot possibilities and shield the area behind you (defend your court).

This principle has wide application in sports. When you are guarding your man in basketball, you have to be very close to him, not 10 feet away. When you are guarding a football receiver, you have to be right on him, not 10 feet away. No matter the sport, as a defender closes in on the guy with the ball, he takes away his angles.

Another benefit of being fully forward is that the net shields your feet. Unless your opponent is fully forward with the ball really

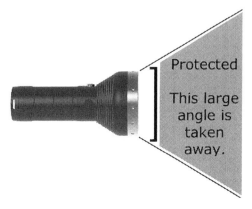

Figure 10-1 Flashlight beam model

high, he can't direct a shot at your feet. Once you back away from the net, your feet become exposed and become targets for shots that will be difficult to return.

The Offensive Advantage of Being Fully Forward

It should also be clear that fully forward represents the best offensive position. From the fully forward position, you can direct shots to almost every location on your opponent's court. Your angles and options are almost unlimited. You can also spike the ball downward.

When you play fully forward you also take time away from your opponent—time that he might need to get back into a good position and time he may need to react to your shot. If you are fully forward and your opponent zaps a fastball at you, you can hit the ball back across the net headed in a new direction in about one sixth of a second. In other words, from the time you make contact with the ball until the time the ball is back across the net is about one sixth of a second. Here's another example. Let's say you are fully forward and your opponent near the baseline hits a shot to you. If you dink the ball back across the net or execute a drop shot, your opponent will have about one half of a second between the time you tap the ball and the time the ball makes a second bounce on his or her side.

Don't Hand Over the Net

Recall point #3 above: If, when on the service receiving team, you fail to secure the net immediately, you will likely allow your opponent to take first control of the net. Here's why. If you fail to get forward, your opponent can hit a rather easy drop shot designed to land just in front of you (called a "keep them back" shot) and then the opponent team will scramble forward to claim the net. At this point, you have handed your opponent a superior court position and your journey to the net will be more difficult.

What Does the Data Show?

How well your team performs in getting fully forward quickly and reliably and how well your team performs in keeping the other team away from the net are strong predictors of rally outcome and game outcome. A review of more than 30 tournament games shows that the team with the best performance in getting fully forward fast will be the winning team about 75 percent of the time.

Among top 5.0-rated players, the third shot alone has a 17 percent chance of directly causing the loss of the rally for the serving team, usually by going into the net, getting smashed back, or getting volleyed back toward the feet. This figure jumps to 27 percent for 4.5-rated players. When players facing a skilled net team fail to get forward or choose not to get forward, they have a 70 percent chance of losing the rally.

If, for Team A, their third shot alone leads directly to a loss of the rally 30 percent of the time, this gives the opponent team, Team B, a 65 percent probability of winning the rally when Team A is serving.

Another study of tournament outcomes found that teams that make no effort to come fully forward or stop their opponents from doing so have essentially no chance of success against teams that employ such strategies.

Wait a Minute! We Don't Play Like This!

I know what many of you are thinking: "I don't know where this comes from, but nobody plays like this. We don't hit soft third shots or dink the ball." Indeed, the strategy discussed is unlike what takes place in most social/recreational play.

Here's how typical recreational play proceeds. The serve is made and the return of serve is made. Usually the weaker opponent is targeted for most shots. The third shot is made in the same way as the return of serve shot is made, perhaps targeting the weaker player. The third shot of the game usually sets off a volley war because the service return team can usually volley this shot back. From this point on, it's just a game of "whack and react." If the ball happens to bounce or slow down, aggression will start again with the next hit. In social play, one main strategy is used: hit the ball hard at the weaker opponent. The good players are the ones who do not flub their shots; they are the players who can hit the ball hard and get it over the net. The bad players are the ones who flub the ball and can't react fast enough in the volley wars. The game is won by the team with the good players—the players who don't flub. If a really good player is involved, you do everything possible to keep the ball away from him or her.

What's the matter with this strategy? Why does anything need to change? It doesn't have to change if you never plan to leave the social/recreational arena. However, you will win more rallies if you do use the "at the line" strategies described in this book. You will have to change if you wish to be competitive against good players who use the at the line strategy. Here's why.

When you use a third shot that looks just like a return of serve shot against a good net team, they will smash it, or, if it's low, they will volley it to a tough location you may not be able to reach. Such third shots do not work against good players. And, on the flip side, if your opponents can make the good third shot drop shots, you will not receive attack opportunities.

Please do not think that the at the line or pro strategy described is only relevant to certain levels of play. Getting fully forward fast and keeping your opponents away from the net is a strategy that works at all levels of play.

A Power Player (Banger) Misconception

In typical social play, especially among former tennis players, where all four players on the court are hard-hitting "bangers," the best bangers (the ones who fault the least) will win. This perpetuates the notion that banging is the best strategy and that the key to winning is to be a really good banger. I know all about this because I was the king banger in my town for a long time (too long). This belief will continue until bangers encounter players who have a broader skill set—players who can bang, defend against bangs, and also perform drop shots, volleys, dinks, and other shots. I've never seen a tournament where pure banger-style play was competitive above the 3.5 skill level. Because "getting forward quickly" performance has been shown over and over to be a major factor in game outcome, most skill raters will not assign a rating above 3.5 to a player who cannot place drop shots into the kitchen.

A Recap

To recap, the general basic strategy used by competitors is 1) return the serve, run forward, and have the service receiving team immediately in control of the net, 2) serving team makes slow drop shot into the kitchen to allow the serving team to get fully forward, and 3) with all players fully forward, dink until a put-away opportunity arises.

Notice that when everything goes right, the service receiving team should only need to play one back court ground stroke (the return of serve) before getting fully forward. Also, when everything goes right, the serving team, if successful with the drop shot, should only need to play one back court ground stroke (the third shot drop shot) before getting fully forward, provided they have good speed. Unlike singles tennis, doubles pickleball is not a game of powering the ball baseline to baseline.

CHAPTER 11: BALL SPIN BASICS

Introduction

You may not need to apply spin to the ball to be a good player, but you do need to know how to detect it and respond to it. Beginning in the next chapter, we start talking about the uses of spin for certain shots. If you come from a tennis or table tennis background, you may already know how to detect, apply, and respond to ball spin. Most players will find that adding spin reduces shot consistency, often causing more lost rallies than benefits. The following is a brief introduction to ball spin.

Backspin

Backspin is popular for return of serve shots, drop shots, and dink shots. You apply the spin by "slicing under" the ball. In other words, you hit a glancing strike beneath the center of the ball that makes it spin back or in reverse. A ball with spin tends to swerve in the direction of the spin. In physics, they call it the Magnus effect. So, a ball with backspin tends to float upwards, seeming to somewhat defy gravity. Sometimes the ball continues to rise as it crosses the net. The Magnus effect lessens the effect of gravity and makes the ball land softly. This creates a low bounce and sometimes a skid. When your opponent hits the ball, the ball will kick off of his or her paddle in the direction of the spin (downward).

When you apply backspin to the return of serve shot, it makes the next shot, the third shot, even more difficult because the player must compensate for the spin or else the ball will dive into the net. When you apply backspin to a drop shot (a drop volley), it helps "float" the ball over the net and it helps stop the ball from going forward where your opponent can better reach it. When you apply backspin to a dink, it helps stop the forward motion of the ball, keeping the ball close to the net. Backspin can also throw off your opponent's timing slightly and help create a fault. Backspin is rather easy to apply with either forehand or backhand strokes. Most backhand shots have some "natural" backspin.

Here's how to handle backspin. First, you need to detect it from your opponent's slicing under the ball paddle action. Next, expect a low bounce and get beneath the ball. To avoid having the ball kick low off of your paddle, you must lift the ball more than usual. Also, it may help to hit the ball well after its apex to help allow the spin to die and to remind you that you need a very upward hit.

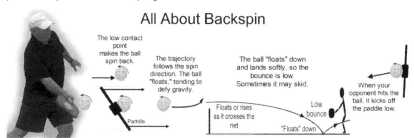

Figure 11-1 All about backspin

Topspin

Topspin or forward spin is really popular in tennis but not so popular in pickleball. You apply the spin by brushing upwards on the ball. In other words, you hit a glancing, upward strike that lifts the ball and spins it forward. Players often call it "rolling the ball" because it is a roll-forward spin. As said above, a ball with spin tends to swerve in the direction of the spin. So, a ball with topspin tends to dive downward. The hard downward dive creates a hard landing and thus a high bounce. The forward spin also makes the ball jump forward. When your opponent hits the ball, the ball will kick off of his or her paddle in the direction of the spin (upward).

In tennis, topspin has a huge virtue: it lets you hit the ball really hard, with the downward swerve protecting the ball from going out of bounds deep. In addition, in tennis, the high bounce and forward kick forces your opponent to stay deep. In pickleball, from the NVZ line, you can use topspin to roll the ball for a down-the-middle shot or you can use it for rolling the ball straight at your opponent (a body shot). These shots are discussed later in the book. The topspin allows putting more power on these shots because the spin will help hold the shots in bounds (making the ball swerve down). Another application for topspin in pickleball is the third shot drive, discussed later. Topspin lets you hit this shot with power while protecting it from going out of bounds. Some players apply topspin to their serves, causing the ball to shoot high and forward after the bounce. When topspin is applied to a lob, it helps the lob stay in bounds and then, after the bounce, it shoots the ball high and forward, making the defender play the shot far behind the baseline.

Here's how to handle topspin. First, you detect it from the brushing upward or "coming over the ball" action of the opponent who hit it. Next, you have to expect the shot to bounce high and jump forward. When topspin is applied to a serve, you need to back up to handle it. When facing heavy topspin, advanced players sometimes hit the ball on the rise (hit a half volley) to avoid getting pushed deep. In all cases of topspin, realize that the ball could come off of your paddle face a little higher than nor-

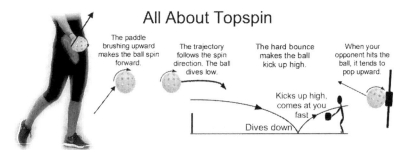

Figure 11-2 All about topspin

mal. When heavy topspin is applied, shots that would normally fly out of bounds may stay in bounds.

I personally don't like to use topspin except when rolling the ball from the NVZ line or when making a defensive lob. Getting a good result from applying topspin requires near-perfect timing.

Sidespin

Sidespin is rarely used in pickleball. However, some folks use it when serving. The best way to deal with it is to return the serve toward the middle of the court, away from the sidelines. Some misdirection shots have sidespin. Again, the best way to deal with it is to avoid returning the shot near sidelines. Sometimes side spin accompanies backspin on return of serve shots. With these, the ball may jump to the side after the bounce in the direction from which your opponent started his or her stroke. As you have a combination of backspin and sidespin, provide a little more lift on your return and stay away from the sidelines.

Unknown spin

I think it's smart to always assume the ball could be carrying spin. That's why you need to leave a margin for error on most shots, especially those near sidelines. You can train your eye to watch the holes in the wiffle ball. If you can see the holes clearly and see that the ball is not rotating, you can surmise that the ball essentially has no spin. If you can't see the holes, assume there is spin and allow a margin for error.

CHAPTER 12: GROUND STROKES AND THE RETURN OF SERVE

Introduction

A ground stroke is a forehand or backhand shot that is executed after the ball bounces once on the court. A volley refers to a strike of the ball before it touches the ground. Ground strokes are either forehand ground strokes or backhand ground strokes. Ground strokes are usually made from either an open stance (i.e., the feet are roughly parallel to the net) or from a closed stance (i.e., the stance is roughly sideways to or perpendicular to the net).

Most dinking shots are ground strokes. However, dinking ground strokes differ from back court ground strokes. Dinking strokes are covered in Chapter 18.

Recall that back court ground strokes are usually only needed once or twice per rally, as most shots will be dinks and volleys. For example, the service receiving team should only need to play one back court ground stroke (the return of serve) before both team members are fully forward.

The Return of Serve Shot

As the service shot must land inside the proper box, the return of serve will always be a ground stroke, never a volley. Most often, the return of serve shot will be a forehand ground stroke, which, in this case, should be executed from a closed or square stance. Wait for the serve about two feet behind the baseline. If your opponent has a very fast and deep serve or a serve with topspin, you may have to wait five or six feet behind the baseline, but be on the lookout for a short serve. Even an extremely fast serve slows down quickly as it descends following the bounce. You should never fault on returning a serve as a result of being too far forward.

The Forehand Ground Stroke Executed from Closed Position

Whether you are talking about golf, baseball, tennis, or racquetball, almost all sports that involve hitting a ball require that you stand sideways to the target (closed position). This closed position provides the most hitting power and the best accuracy. It permits a full coil and uncoil of the upper body. Hitting from a closed position puts the impact point at about the center of the swing path and at about the highest point of racquet, bat, or club velocity. For example, in golf, the club head speed is highest at about the point of impact. In golf, it has been well established that being perfectly sideways or "square" to the target also yields the best accuracy.

Now let's talk about movement into position. When waiting to receive the serve, you should be behind the baseline, usually about two feet behind, and facing the server (open to, not sideways to, the server). A mistake is to be too far forward such that you have to "dig out" a shot at your feet or travel backwards to get into position to hit the shot. A beginner mistake is "getting jammed at the baseline," faulting from trying to dig a shot at the feet because you were too far forward.

If your backhand shots are weak, you may slightly bias your positioning to the left (for a right-handed player) to help ensure that most serves will come to your forehand side. As you are at least 44 feet from the server, you should have time to react and get into position, even if the serve is fast. If the ball is essentially coming right to you, you may only need to pivot to swing your body into place. See Figure 12-1. If you must move laterally (i.e., to the side), the best foot-work is a side shuffle step versus a cross-ing step. If you must move forward, a for-ward shuffle or gal-lop step is preferable to a running step.

If you must move backwards, a back-to-

Pivot to Forehand   Pivot to Backhand

Figure 12-1 Position to allow pivoting to either fore-hand or backhand

gether-back (backwards gallop step) is preferable to running backwards (back pedaling). Of course sometimes you must scramble, run, and sometimes "hit on the run." However, to the extent possible, you need to move into position quickly and execute your return of serve shot from a stable stance. Hitting from a stable stance is a key need in pickleball. Most peo-ple think they have more control than they really do. To get the ball to go where you want it to go, you have to be able to aim the paddle and move it forward in a linear path through the strike. You can't do that very well while running. Also, most pickleball shots are low shots, because the ball does not bounce high. You can't hit low shots with consistency if you are trying to hit them while running.

Coach Mo frequently uses the analogy of a hunter trying to fire a gun. A hunter never tries to aim and shoot while running. In order to aim and get an accurate shot, the hunter must be completely stable, aiming while motionless. The same applies to pickleball.

The correct "setup," that is, the correct ball positioning relative to your stance, is as follows. First, the ball should be in front of you. Specif-ically, the ball should be as far forward as your lead toe at the moment of the strike. As you need not attack with the return of serve, you need not seek to hit the ball at its apex. So, seek to have a setup where your impact occurs as the ball is descending. Next, the ball should be close enough to you to ensure that your upper arm can remain close to your body. Your shot consistency degrades rapidly if you must reach out to hit the ball. You must also bend your knees and lower yourself to meet the ball. It's in this point where you see a striking difference between great players and social players. Social players rarely bend their knees or lower to meet the ball. Top players will get very low when the ball is low. As the for-

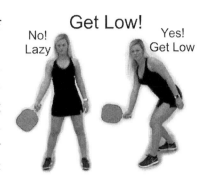

Figure 12-2 Get low!

ward paddle movement is made, you must transfer your weight forward in the direction of the ball path. If you can, it's helpful to step forward into the stroke with your left foot (for a right-handed player) and con-tact the ball opposite the location of your forward toe. Time the step so that you step just before making contact so that your momentum goes into the shot.

Setting up the Swing: The Unit Turn

Now let's talk about the first part of the swing called the unit turn. In the ready position, you should have both hands on the paddle. The unit turn involves keeping both hands on the paddle and turning the body and paddle in unison as you are moving and getting into the forehand stance.

Professional tennis players do this automatically from their years of training and practice. A mistake is to swing the paddle back independently of the upper body. This mistake cre-ates a huge misalignment between your shoulders and the swing path.

The unit turn essentially com-pletes the back swing, sets the paddle face to the correct aiming position, and sets up for the forward stroke,

Figure 12-3 The unit turn

which is rather linear as if hitting four balls in a row. During the unit turn, the left hand assists in setting the paddle to the proper target direction. At the conclusion of the unit turn, that is, at the full backswing position, the paddle will be aimed at the target trajectory, and usually about parallel to the net. After setting the paddle, keep the left hand out in front, at the same height as your hitting hand, with the palm facing the ground. This helps keep you in a balanced position.

I urge players to avoid letting the paddle face drop below the wrist. Instead, I recommend having the paddle cocked up enough so that you can see wrinkles in your skin at the wrist. Usually this means you will have to bend your knees quite a bit to meet the ball in a way that avoids dropping the paddle head. Coach Mo often says, "Pretend you are sitting in a chair with your nose down at the height of the ball."

The Forward Swing

Suppose you were using the pointer paddle described earlier, where the antenna points to the exact direction where the ball should travel. At the conclusion of the unit turn described above, the antenna and paddle face should be set and the antenna should be pointing to the intended ball flight path. If all of this is correctly set, the forward motion of the paddle as it travels toward impact stays in line with the antenna through impact as if hitting four balls in a row. Coach Mo teaches folks that at the end of this stroke (after follow through), you should be able to kiss your bicep muscle. Unlike in tennis, the pickleball paddle follow through should not circle around your body. When teaching, Coach Mo says to avoid the Merry-Go-Round motion. Instead, he suggests the Ferris wheel image.

As the weight shifts forward during the stroke, or if you step out during the stroke, this forward momentum adds to the stroke. This moving forward action adds power and can also help keep your stroke more linear and less curving. See Figure 12-4. Do not pop up, lift your head, or abruptly straighten your knees during the stroke.

Watching the Ball

Everybody knows you are supposed to watch the ball. However, most folks do not watch the ball all the way through contact. Instead, they lift their head, look forward too early, and mis-hit as a result. Coach Mo teaches players to make a sound, even if faint, at the exact moment of contact, as a way to ensure that they are watching the ball through contact, not moving their eyes away

Figure 12-4 Forward momentum adds to the stroke and helps keep your stroke more linear

from the contact point until after the ball is gone. Coach Mo uses the expression "sound like a pro," which means make a sound the way the pro tennis players do when they contact the ball.

Watching the ball all the way to the paddle is another thing you can practice with a wall. If you watch slow motion videos of the top pro tennis players you will see that they watch the ball all the way to the strings, not "peeking" until the ball is long gone.

Photo Sequences of the Forehand Ground Stroke

Please refer to the following photos to study the key points.

Forehand Ground Stroke: Aiming the Paddle

Key Points: 1) Continental grip with wrist firm and cocked up, 2) elbow tight to the body and slightly bent, 3) lead shoulder pointing toward the incoming

Forehand Ground Stroke Aiming the Paddle

Figure 12-5 Forehand ground stroke: aiming the paddle

85

ball, 4) back straight, 5) eyes watching the incoming ball, 6) paddle level or above the wrist with face open and aimed, 7) knees bent to prevent dipping the paddle head, 8) feet about shoulder width apart, 9) use left hand to assist pushing paddle into place near the left toe.

Forehand Ground Stroke: Stepping Out, Contact Point

Forehand Ground Stroke
Stepping Out, Contact Point

Figure 12-6 Forehand ground stroke: stepping out, contact point

Key Points: 1) Continental grip, wrist firm and tilted up, 2) upper arm close to body, 3) lead shoulder points toward the ball, 4) back straight, 5) eyes watch the ball through contact, 6) aimed paddle moves forward to front toe contact point, 7) head stays down until after contact, 8) bend knees to get beneath the ball and to keep the paddle head from dipping, 9) left foot steps forward into the strike.

Forehand Ground Stroke: Follow Through

Forehand Ground Stroke
Follow Through

Figure 12-7 Forehand ground stroke: follow through

Key Points: 1) notice the paddle face is still pointed toward the target, not wrapping around, 2) the elbow is fully extended toward the target, 3) the eyes are still looking at the contact point, the head remains down, and you should be able to kiss your bicep, 4) the line through the feet will usually match the line of flight.

Low Forehand Ground Stroke: Follow Through
Key Points: 1) the paddle face is still pointed toward the target, not wrapping around, 2) the elbow is fully extended toward the tar-

Low Forehand Ground Stroke Follow Through

get, 3) the eyes are still looking at the contact point, the
head remains down, and you
should be able to kiss your
bicep, 4) the line through
the feet will usually match
the line of flight, 5) knees
are bent, 6) the left hand is
expended toward the target,
palm down for balance.

Figure 12-8 Low forehand ground stroke: follow through

The Backhand Ground Stroke Executed from Closed Position

Let's say the serve is coming to your backhand. Most players, especially if they have no prior tennis experience, struggle with backhand shots. If your backhand is weak, position yourself slightly left when waiting for the serve. This should ensure more shots come to your forehand side. If the serve is coming to your backhand, and if it is slow enough, quickly side shuffle (or run if necessary) to the left so that you can hit a forehand shot. (This is called running around to the forehand.) On serve returns, even many good players do this to allow optimal returns. Don't worry about getting out of position or far away from your partner. Here's why. The serving team will have to wait for your return of serve to bounce before they can hit the ball. If you return the serve with a rather slow semi-lob, you should have plenty of time to get fully forward to the NVZ line and be "re-connected" to your partner. Note: returning the serve is about the only time you can safely run around to the forehand, as you have plenty of time to recover a good court position. In advanced pickleball play, most shots are volleys and dinks and most will be executed with the backhand. So, you will need to practice and develop backhand skill.

Now let's say a fast serve is coming to your backhand and making a backhand ground stroke return is unavoidable. Here's how to handle it.

The backhand ground stroke has almost all of the elements and steps of the forehand ground stroke. They are essentially the same, except on the backhand stroke, your non-paddle hand moves back for balance, whereas on the forehand ground stroke, your non-paddle hand is placed in front of your body for balance. Specifically:

1. Begin by being in the compressed, ready position behind the baseline facing (not perpendicular to) the server with both hands on the paddle.

2. Pivot or shuffle to get perpendicular to the target, making the unit turn, and getting positioned so the ball is as far forward as the lead toe, and so the ball is descending, and so that your upper arm can stay close to your body to avoid reaching out.

3. Bend the knees and get low enough to meet and lift the ball.

4. At the end of the unit turn, set the paddle face to point to the start of the desired ball flight path.

5. Using weight shift forward body action or stepping out into the shot movement, upper body uncoiling action, and a little bit of movement from the shoulder, push the paddle forward through impact along the flight path line as if hitting four balls in a row. Step into the shot when you can, stepping out just before making contact and timing the step so that your momentum goes into the strike, as when hitting a baseball.

Backhand Ground Stroke Aiming the Paddle

Figure 12-9 Backhand ground stroke: aiming the paddle

Photo Sequences of the Backhand Ground Stroke

Backhand Ground Stroke: Aiming the Paddle
Key Points: 1) Continental grip, wrist firm, paddle tilted up, 2) left hand helps aim the paddle face, 3) the paddle face is aimed at the

target trajectory, 4) knees are bent to get beneath the ball, 5) the eyes watch the ball all the way through contact.

Backhand Ground Stroke: Follow Through
Key Points: 1) wrist firm, paddle tilted up, 2) paddle face still points at target and does not go around the body, 3) elbow moves to full extension toward target, 4) head stays down and eyes watch the ball all the way through contact, 5) lead shoulder, feet, and paddle point to the target.

Backhand Ground Stroke: Contact Point
Key Points: 1) feet and paddle point to the target, 2) lead shoulder points to target and contact point is even with the forward toe, 3) left hand extends back for balance, 4) knees bend so that you can get under the ball and not drop the paddle head.

Low Backhand Ground Stroke: Follow Through
Key Points: 1) head stays down, 2) eyes are still looking at the contact point and you should be able to kiss your bicep, 3) elbow is at full extension toward the target, 4) the paddle face has not rotated but is toward the target (Note that the stroke is linear and toward the target. It does not wrap around the body.), 5) the knees stay bent until follow-through has been completed.

Backhand Ground Stroke Follow Through

Figure 12-10 Backhand ground stroke: follow through

Backhand Ground Stroke Contact Point

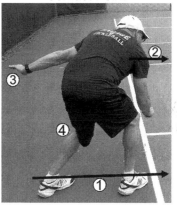

Figure 12-11 Backhand ground stroke: contact point

Backspin Returns

Advanced players frequently add backspin to their return of serve shots. Even if you know how to deal with spin, this still makes the already tricky third shot even more difficult. Unfortunately, adding backspin adds to your risk of faulting on the return of serve, adds to your risk of making short returns, and adds to the risk that you may not get fully forward in time to receive the third shot.

Low Backhand Ground Stroke Follow Through

Figure 12-12 Low backhand ground stroke: follow through

However, if you are good at adding spin, and can get forward fast after making the shot, the rewards often outweigh the risks. Players who don't know how to compensate for the backspin dump their shots into the net.

The stroke technique for the backspin return of serve is like the technique for the drop volley (drop shot) discussed later. Don't chop or hack downward. Instead, use the classic quarter-moon-shaped stroke that tennis players use. See Figure 12-13.

Figure 12-13 Back spin return of serve

How to Handle Backspin Return of Serve Shots

If your opponent applies backspin and you do not compensate for the backspin, your third shot will likely go into the net. When you see that backspin has been applied, hit the ball well after its apex (as it is descending) and hit upward, applying additional lift. This requires some practice and experience.

The Goals, Objectives, and Strategy of a Service Return

The goals of a service return are:

1. *Go to the weakness.* Try to return the ball to whichever opponent is less skillful with the critical third shot drop shot. Further, go to his or her worst side (usually the backhand side). If both players are about equal in skill, hit directly between them but closer to the left opponent, forcing a low-to-the-backhand return. This forces at least some movement or stress, thus making the third shot a little more difficult than a shot requiring no movement. This down-the-middle shot also has the advantage of going over the lowest part of the net and possibly causing confusion between your opponents about who will field the shot. See Figure 12-14.

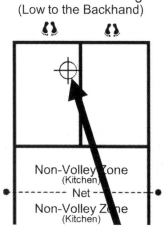

Service Return Target
(Low to the Backhand)

Figure 12-14 Service return target

2. *Gives you time.* Make sure your return gives you enough time to get fully forward to the NVZ line before the next shot comes back. This is vital in order to quickly return the third shot, volleying it if possible, to stop your opponents' forward progress. It's also vital for forcing your opponent to play the very difficult critical third shot. Getting to the line on time gives you a chance to smash or attack a third shot that is attackable. Such attackable third shots are very frequent in social play. If you are slow or otherwise have limited mobility, use a lob or semi-lob to return the serve so that you can get to the line on time. I like to hit a semi-lob so that I have plenty of time to get forward. I also like to contact the ball near the base of my paddle (near the handle). I feel that this contact location gives me good control of the placement distance.

After hitting the return of serve shot, you and your partner need to "converge on the ball," staying linked, and centering the defensive wall according to the ball location. See Figure 12-15.

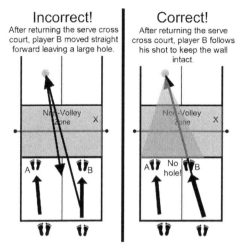

Figure 12-15 Correct positioning after returning the serve

3. *Deep, but not real deep.* Try to get the return of serve to land in the back half of your opponents' court. If you return the serve short, it could invite a fastball attack. You don't need your shot to be fast, just deep, but not really deep near the baseline. You must allow a margin for error.

4. *Do not fault.* Most faults result from trying to get aggressive with the return of serve shot. Do not try to "hit a winner," or hit a fastball, or issue a low-to-the-net ball. In pickleball, the service return team has the strategic advantage because they should have the first control of the net. The failure rate of the serving team in their struggle to get fully forward is usually greater than 20 percent. So, all else being equal, the service return team should have at least a 60 percent chance of winning each time they can get the serve returned successfully. Do not squander this advantage by faulting on a rather simple return of serve shot.

5. *Add difficulty to the third shot if you can.* If you can reliably put backspin on the ball without compromising the other four goals above, do so. When the service receiver puts spin on his or her shot it makes the already tricky third shot even more difficult.

Mistakes to Avoid

1. **Trying to win the rally with the return of serve.** The common mistake that characterizes almost all players below the 4.0 skill level is that they try to "win the point" (hit the ball hard) with every shot they hit. They unwisely start aggression before they are fully forward. Returning the serve is not the time to try to win the rally.

2. **Not getting fully forward.** The next mistake that many 4.0 and below players make is that they return the serve but then fail to get fully forward before the next shot (i.e., the third shot) comes across the net, thereby giving their opponent an easier third shot and missing attack opportunities. Huge mistake.

Pickleball Commandment Number 2: Never Miss a Return of Serve

You should never fault with a return of serve shot. Consider these three points:

1. As the server is behind one baseline and you are behind the other, you typically have 44 feet of ball flight time to get ready.
2. You normally only have to move a step or two to get to the ball.
3. As your shot must bounce before being hit, you have the entire opponent court open to receive your shot. Playing situations are seldom more generous than this. Again, the return of serve team has at least a 60 percent probability of winning the rally. Do not squander your opportunity by botching a simple return of serve shot.

Making it Happen

1. Anybody who wants to get good at pickleball or stay good at pickleball needs a practice partner or practice wall or both. Even if you have a tennis background, you need to practice the above forehand and backhand sequences to make them smooth and automatic. Have your practice partner repeatedly hit deep shots

to your forehand and then to your backhand. Later, you can mix them up or alternate the forehand and backhand shots. Do all of the steps above and pick an exact point where you wish to land your shots. Make sure you return to the ready position after each shot. To some extent, you can practice the sequences in your home without having a partner or practice wall.

2. On your next outing, set a goal to return each serve with a slow semi-lob that allows you to get fully forward before the next shot reaches the net.

3. On your next outing, when your partner is receiving the serve, get fully forward and get your toes pinned to the NVZ line before the server hits the ball. You can twist your upper body to observe whether the serve lands in bounds or not.

CHAPTER 13: MOVEMENT, POSITIONING, AND TECHNIQUE SUMMARY

Key Points about Movement and Positioning

1. Be alert, watch your opponent's paddle, and get an early indication of where your opponent plans to hit the ball.

2. If you step into the court when serving, get back out quickly, and stay two feet behind the baseline until you can assess the return of serve. Your partner should also be two feet behind the baseline until the return of serve can be assessed.

3. When waiting for a serve, you may need to stand three feet or more behind the baseline to handle fastball serves and to avoid playing a low half volley. Do not get jammed at the baseline. Note: it is not uncommon for four or more points to be "given away" due only to player positioning mistakes (being too far forward) when waiting for a serve or waiting for a return of serve. Also, it is difficult to make a good third shot if you are retreating while fielding the return of serve.

4. Move into position quickly. When returning the serve and when preparing to hit the third shot, you should have enough time to get into a closed stance (get sideways). Point your shoulder toward your target, and step forward just before contact so that you have forward momentum into the strike.

5. The partner of the service receiver should be fully forward and pinned to the line before the serve is received.

6. Once the return of serve shot is hit, this player needs to get fully forward and compressed at the NVZ line before the third shot arrives.

7. Once you are established, compressed, and leaning in at the NVZ line, nothing but a lob or imminent close-range smash should bring you off of the line. When you are compressed with a forward lean, you should be able to volley back shots coming toward your feet.

8. Whenever you must move laterally, seek to stay facing your opponent and preserve your ready position base as much as possible.

9. When in no man's land, you must stop, split step, and compress every time your opponent touches the ball. Don't sacrifice being stable and ready in order to achieve a slightly better court position.

Key Points about Technique

1. To the extent that you can, move into position quickly in order to provide the best setup possible. In golf, the ball is stationary, allowing you to create an ideal setup. In pickleball, racquetball, and tennis, you must move to the moving ball to the best of your ability to create the setup.

2. Get low and get under the ball so that you can keep the paddle at least horizontal or, even better, above the wrist.

3. Once in place, make the unit turn, aim the paddle, and set it motionless for a moment. Step out and push the paddle straight forward through "four balls in a row." Contact the ball in front of your body, opposite your lead toe. Again, early preparation is important. Avoid wrist action; instead keep the wrist firm through the whole stroke.

4. Watch the ball all the way to the contact point, not peeking until after the ball is gone. To help you stay conscious of this, make a

sound at the exact moment that you see the ball contact the paddle. As Coach Mo advises, "Sound like a pro." Follow through toward the target. Don't pop up but stay low through the entire stroke.

CHAPTER 14: THE CRITICAL THIRD SHOT

Let's say you are on the serving team. Your opponent returned the serve deep into your court. Both opponents are now fully forward and they are linked together. You are certainly at a disadvantage. If you hit a shot that is too soft, it will go into the net. If you hit a shot that is high, they will smash it back. If you hit a net-high shot that they can volley back, they will direct it to a place that is hard for you to reach, which will stop your forward progress. If you continue to stay away from the net while your opponents are fully forward, you will likely lose the rally, as the net players have a strategic advantage.

What do you do? Most coaches and most top players agree on the following strategy.

Option 1: If the return of serve is short and to the forehand (and especially if it has a high bounce), a high-speed down-the-middle drive shot is a good choice if you have skill with this shot. Such a shot can likely only be blocked, which allows your team some forward advancement and, hopefully, an easier fifth shot drop. This drive shot is not so easy. If it's too low, it goes into the net. If it's too high, it goes out of bounds. A drive down the middle is also a good choice if your opponents are not properly linked or are slow getting forward.

Option 2: If the return of serve is rather deep, the third shot drop is usually the best option. This is a tough shot, but a very necessary shot. This rather slow shot gives you time to advance toward the NVZ line. In addition, if the shot drops softly into the kitchen, it will not bounce very high and thus not be very attackable.

Option 3: If the return of serve is really deep or gets you in trouble where you can't set up for making a drop shot, a defensive lob may be the only option left. Note: if you have to do this, go over the left opponent's left shoulder.

Option 2 above, the third shot drop, is the shot played most often.

As discussed in the introduction, the key need for most shots in pickleball is distance control. Let's take a look at the third shot drop.

By far, the most difficult, most critical, and most important shot to master in pickleball is the drop shot into the kitchen. In advanced play, when serving, you must be able to get your team forward reliably. A successful rather slow third shot drop into the kitchen provides some time for the serving team to advance forward. The sooner you learn to make this shot, the better off you will be.

Many otherwise good players fail to understand the vital importance of getting fully forward reliably and as quickly as possible. The data is clear, however. Among equally skilled advanced players, the statistic is this: if the other team is at the NVZ line and you can't get your team there, then you have a 70 percent chance of losing the rally. In advanced-level play, skill in getting forward quickly and reliably is an important determinant in which team wins the match.

You will never get very far in pickleball if you cannot develop this drop shot. So, what's the secret to it? Imagine this challenge. Let's say you are standing at the baseline next to a shopping cart full of pickleballs. Your goal is to toss or throw as many balls into the kitchen as possible. The balls must land (bounce) in the opponent's kitchen area. For each success, you receive $100. For each failure, you pay $100. In such a case, what technique would you use to toss the ball? Almost certainly you would use an underhand toss that approximates the straight release of a bowling ball. Almost certainly you would avoid a wrist flick at the moment of ball release. Instead, you attempt to push the ball along the intended path. Likely, your arm would move as one unit. Most of the arm movement would originate from your weight transfer to your forward foot and from upper body rotation (the shoulders turning). Only a rather small amount comes from rotation of the shoulder.

This is exactly how the third shot drop should be made: like a precision ball toss or straight release of a bowling ball. So, I hold my paddle firmly and I also try to have the ball contact the paddle on the lower part of the paddle (near my hand) so that the effect of any minor wrist action is further minimized. In other words, I want the paddle speed to be the same as the speed of my hand. Further, I try to push the ball as if hitting several balls in a row. Recall from the "pointer paddle" teaching aid that directional control is difficult if the paddle is curving or swinging at the moment of impact.

As the third shot is so difficult, I try to get to my setup position early. I wait for the ball to pass its apex so that it is descending when I make the hit. I also bend my knees to get beneath the ball so that I can lift it. I try to aim early. I also make sure the paddle is aimed so that I am hitting up on the ball, lifting it, and hitting "four balls in a row." When I fail and dump the ball into the net, it's usually because I fail to have enough lift, instead, hitting too flat.

Although the third shot drop is a rather soft shot, you still need to accelerate, at least slightly, through contact. Decelerating or "quitting" on a shot is never a good practice. So, to ensure acceleration, I think about popping the ball through the strike, even if it's a small pop.

To be good with the third shot drop, you must define and replicate the angle, speed, and paddle path needed for success. In golf, you are trained to stop thinking about hitting the ball and start thinking about making a good swing. The advice is to let the ball get in the way of your good swing. I think this advice applies to the third shot. You must apply a good and consistent stroke to get a good and consistent outcome.

Another key point is that the desired trajectory is such that the ball is falling or descending as it crosses the net. So the trajectory apex is on your side of the court, not the opponents' side.

Many players try the drop shot a few times, experience failure, and quickly give up trying to use it. This is unfortunate as mastering this shot is what enables good players to become great players. I think that patience through just a few practice sessions

Figure 14-1 To be good with the third shot drop, you must define and replicate the angle, speed, and paddle path needed for success

can build the skill required to allow you to use this shot in your regular play.

The Social Play Situation

Many social/recreational players blow off the whole notion of the soft third shot. The attitude is that this does not apply to their style of play. I disagree. In social/recreational play, about half of the rallies end with only four or fewer shots taken. I realize this sounds unbelievable. But, after the serve and return of serve, about half of rallies end with only two additional hits made. About two-thirds of rallies end with five or fewer hits.

Most players would agree that the serve and the return of serve should be rather easy, straightforward shots. Why do so many rallies fall apart and end two or three shots later?

The main culprit is the third shot (the return of the return of serve), which either ends or starts to end the rally. At this level of play, the third shot will lead directly to a loss of the rally for 40–50 percent of the rallies. Here's what usually happens. In preparing to receive the serve, the service return team has one player fully forward or almost fully forward. After returning the serve, this player then advances forward. This team now has both players forward or somewhere near the front of the box. Next, the serving team typically hits a third shot that looks just like a return of serve shot. However, their opponents are forward and they can attack this third shot. If the third shot is high, it can be smashed. Even if it's not very high, it can be smacked toward the feet of the incoming opponents. Among 3.0–3.5 rated players, the third shot can almost always be volleyed and so these net players smack the ball at their opponents, who are stuck somewhere deep in the court.

As I said above, the main culprit is the third shot—specifically, a third shot hit hard enough and high enough so that it sets off a volley war. The key need is for the third shot to bounce before being hit. So, don't try to win the rally with the third shot. Instead, go soft. A pickleball that bounces is low and not very attackable. How do we make that happen?

In typical social play, your opponents are not usually fully forward or they are slow getting forward. So, as you are making the third shot, your opponents are probably somewhere in no man's land. This allows you to make a rather easy third shot that need not bounce in the kitchen; instead, it can bounce just somewhere in front of your opponent. Again, the key need for the third shot is for it to bounce before your opponent hits it. This allows you time to get forward and it keeps the ball from being attackable. So, when your opponents are not fully forward, aim for the left heel target or somewhere just in front of the left heel target. Do not give your opponent a volley shot as most volleys are attackable and they stop your forward progress. Giving an easy volley shot to an opponent in a superior court position is dumb (low percentage) play, not smart play. When your opponents are not fully forward, don't try to drop the shot into the kitchen. Such a shot is difficult and it draws your opponents forward into a better court position. Hit your third shot as shown in Figure 14-2. An ideal time to practice the third shot drop is when the return of serve is short. From this close distance, the third shot is just a slightly long dink.

Among otherwise equally skilled players at the advanced intermediate (3.5) level, rally outcome mainly hinges on the quality of the third shot, specifically on how attackable the third shot is. Likewise, the game outcome will mainly depend on which team provides the least number of attackable third shots.

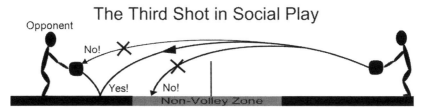

Figure 14-2 *The third shot in social play*

Other Third Shot Options

1. If a return of serve is short and coming to your forehand, a low drive shot straight down the middle can be a good choice. Such a shot can sometimes be a winner. If not, it would normally be blocked, hopefully allowing you to dink the blocked shot into the kitchen.

2. If your opponents are a little sluggish getting forward and are not tightly linked together, a drive shot down the middle can sometimes be a winner or cause a weak return. This situation occurs frequently in social play.

3. Let's say your opponents are great net players who get in place fast and penalize you for every third shot drop mistake. Your third shot drop attempts are just not working. They are either going too high and getting attacked or they are going into the net. This is often how mid-level players feel when they are playing against advanced players. Every time you get to serve you lose it due to third shot faults. In such a case, a three-quarter speed low drive straight down the centerline could be your best option. Such a shot could likely be volleyed back, but not attacked. You will likely get stuck in no man's land for a while, but at least you have kept the ball in play.

4. Get help from your partner. Let's say the net team is tough and your third shot drop attempts are just not working. You could ask your partner to take shots that should belong to you.

5. You are in trouble and cannot make a good third shot. Let's say you have gotten into trouble, backing up or hitting on the run.

For whatever reason, you do not think you can make a good third shot. In such a case, you may need to lob. Send the lob over the left opponent's left shoulder (just left of the centerline) so that your opponent has to use a backhand shot.

6. A popular advanced strategy is to hit a third shot drive and then have your more forward partner attempt to poach the block to make a put-away shot. For this to work you and your partner need to coordinate and practice the sequence. By the way, to defend against this strategy, try to return the serve to player backhands and block the drive back so that it lands low and away from the potential poacher or to a backhand.

An Advanced Technique: Making the Drop Shot from a Half Volley

I think most players will find it easier to execute and replicate a shot if they hit the ball as it descends after its apex. At this point, the ball has lost speed and the upward hit will be in line with the downward trajectory preceding the hit. An advanced technique is to hit the third shot from the "short hop" (hit a half volley third shot). This short hop shot requires skill and practice but it can be beneficial for two reasons. First, by hitting the ball just after the bounce, it gets you closer to the net and makes your third shot shorter. Second, if your opponent is a little slow in getting forward, the short hop shot can likely bounce before being hit, even if it lands outside the kitchen. This technique works best when the return of serve shot is rather short, not when the return of serve lands near the baseline.

Practice Drills

Partner Practice Third Shot Drill

Here's an easy drill you can do with a practice partner to help you develop the third shot drop. Facing your practice partner with both of you fully forward at the NVZ line, dink the ball back and forth. Slowly move deeper in the court, keeping your practice partner in place at the line. Keep trying to drop your shots into the kitchen as you move further away from the kitchen, and eventually to the baseline. Keep mental notes of the exact stroke that works, including the paddle speed and loft. Notice that the ball should descend as it crosses the net. The apex of the trajectory is well in front of the net. Of course, shots that go over a little too high are better than those that go into the net. Practice both forehand and backhand. You should be able to develop the feel for the shot and know, as soon as you hit the shot, if it will be good or bad.

Allow your partner to practice the shot also. As this shot is so important, your practice partner will likely enjoy this drill. To create a challenge, see how many shots in a row you can drop into the kitchen. A goal is to find the stroke that works, try to define it, and then groove it into muscle memory.

Ball Toss Drill

Using an underhand softball pitching motion, try to toss a pickleball into the NVZ. This will help you learn the required upward motion stroke technique and the needed speed and trajectory. Move to different locations and repeat the toss.

Third Shot Wall Drill

There's also a backboard wall drill that you can use to develop this shot. If the wall is not marked to show a net, place a piece of painter's tape at net height to simulate the top of the net tape. Stand about 20 feet back from the wall. First, hit the ball rather hard and high at the wall so that the return bounce brings the ball back to your location (20 feet from the wall). Next, try to hit the drop shot so that the ball descends as it hits the wall. Try to hit the wall about two feet above the tape. As the ball returns to you, it will bounce 2–3 times before getting back to your location. After its second or third bounce, again hit the ball rather high and hard at the wall to repeat the pattern. Notice, you can only practice the drop shot every other time you hit the ball.

The Third Shot Drop: Goals, Objective, and Strategy

The ideal third shot drop has these characteristics:

1. **Cannot be volleyed back,** but bounces before your opponent hits it. This is a key need.

2. **Goes deep if your opponents are deep.** When they are back, keep them back! Try to have your third shot bounce just in front of their feet. If an opponent routinely fails to get fully forward on time for the third shot, place your third shot just in front of him and toward his backhand.

3. **Has a rather low bounce.** If the shot has too much loft and creates a high bounce, it could invite a fastball return, which could be tough to handle.

4. **Goes to a player's backhand, not forehand.** This way, if the shot is too high or bounces too high, you avoid receiving a strong forehand response.

Third Shot Targets

I usually try to place the third shot drop close (but not too close) to the sideline at the right opponent's backhand (for a right-handed opponent on the right side). If the left player is weaker, I may try to go to the left player's backhand. A place to avoid is the right opponent's forehand, which is in the center (for a right-handed player). Even a good third shot drop will usually be more attackable than a typical dink. So, if your down-the-center third shot has a high bounce or bounces near the NVZ line, you could receive a strong forehand attack. I think players who are intermediate and below should aim for Target 2 in order to stay away from the sidelines.

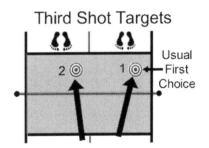

Figure 14-3 Third shot targets

Get Forward

Of course, the purpose of the rather slow third shot drop is to allow your team to advance. You have all of the ball flight time plus all of the time between the bounce and the hit to advance. A serious mistake is to hit a great third shot and then fail to make every bit of forward progress possible. Great players push off their back foot and move forward into the strike, using this motion to begin forward progress. Most 5.0-rated players are disappointed if they can't get fully to the NVZ line after making a good third shot drop. At a minimum, you should get halfway through no man's land toward the NVZ line following a good drop shot.

Common Mistakes

1. **Being too far forward when waiting for the return of serve, thus getting jammed or requiring backwards movement.** You need to wait behind the baseline until you can assess the return of serve shot. It's nearly impossible to hit a great third shot if your momentum is carrying you backwards.
2. **Hitting a third shot just like a return of serve shot.** This is by far the most frequent third shot mistake. You are deep in the court and you are giving your opponents at the net an easy volley shot that they can smack back at you or your feet.
3. **Slowing down your current stroke.** If you try to make a third shot drop by taking your current ground stroke shot and slowing it down, you will dump your shots into the net. When you slow down the swing, you must provide more lift. You must get beneath the ball, the paddle path must be low to high, your paddle must be open, adding loft, and you need to have forward momentum and acceleration into the strike.

Other Perspectives

There are many great YouTube videos made by top pickleball professionals that show techniques for shots such as the third shot drop.

Comments

Almost all social/recreational pickleball players play a style of pickleball I call "Whack and React." Once the ball is served, everybody goes into full aggression, whacking and reacting. Usually the rally ends with the serving team never getting fully forward. A regret of mine is not learning the third shot and the rather simple strategy of playing "at-the-line" pickleball sooner than I did. A whole new level of enjoyment comes from playing strategies that are only used when all players are fully forward.

Of the many hundreds or maybe thousands of pickleball games that I have played, I can distinctly remember the exact game that made me decide that from that point forward I would use and practice the third shot drop. I somehow got invited into a game consisting of 4.5–5.0-rated players. I had a great partner, but we got killed as a result of my lousy third shot choices. Needless to say I did not get invited back. However, within a few weeks (and after about six hours of third shot practice), I had a respectable third shot and my winning percentages improved dramatically.

Making it Happen

No matter what level of play you are involved in, the best third shot is one that bounces before your opponent can hit it. When you can make such a shot and then follow it to get your team forward, you maximize your chances of winning the rally. On your next outing, try to avoid hitting your third shot such that your opponent can volley it back. If you can't remember the left heel target, seek to place the ball at the toes of your opponent or halfway between where the left opponent is standing and where the right opponent is standing. Such shots are difficult to "dig out." Follow your third shot and get to the NVZ line if possible.

CHAPTER 15: THIRD SHOT DEFENSIVE STRATEGIES AND THE FOURTH SHOT

Defending Against the Third Shot

Let's say your opponents are trying to hit a third shot drop shot into the kitchen. First of all, you and your teammate should be fully forward at the NVZ line before any third shot from your opponents comes across the net. It's a serious mistake to be late to the line or to not be fully forward. It's only when you are fully forward, and fully forward on time, that you force your opponents to play the very most difficult version of the "critical third shot." Here's what game analysis data clearly shows. At the top (5.0) skill level, problems with the third shot (e.g., too high, faulting into the net) lead directly to a loss of the rally for the serving team in one out of five rallies (a 20 percent failure rate). This gives the service return team 60/40 odds of winning the rally. At lower skill levels, the service return team has an even larger advantage. However, this advantage is only realized if the service return team is fully forward on time so that they force the serving team to hit the difficult third shot drop or suffer the consequences of hitting a shot that can be volleyed back. Again, the advantage is lost or diminished if you fail to get fully forward before the third shot comes across the net. Here are the reasons why.

1. When you fail to get fully forward or you are late getting fully forward, you give your opponent a much easier third shot, providing him a large window where his shot can arrive and bounce in front

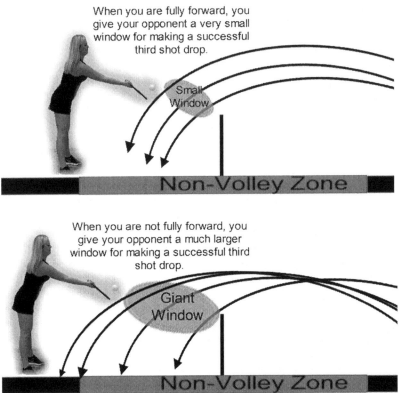

The Importance of Getting Fully Forward On Time Every Time

When you are fully forward, you give your opponent a very small window for making a successful third shot drop.

Small Window

Non-Volley Zone

When you are not fully forward, you give your opponent a much larger window for making a successful third shot drop.

Giant Window

Non-Volley Zone

Figure 15-1 The importance of getting fully forward on time, every time

of you. When you are fully forward, the window where the shot can arrive and bounce in front of you is small. One of the most important factors determining the outcome of advanced-level play is your team's performance in keeping control of the net and keeping your opponents away from it. You must make your opponents' quest to get forward as difficult as possible.

2. When you fail to get fully forward or you are late getting fully forward, you miss offensive opportunities such as being able to volley the ball back or smash it back. Sometimes missing a volley opportunity creates a very difficult defensive shot.

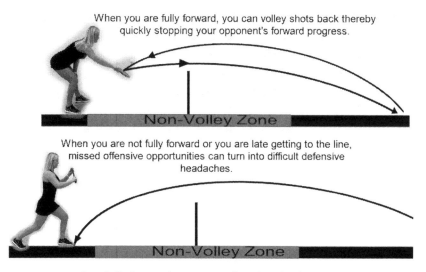

Figure 15-2 When fully forward, you can volley shots back

Defending Against a Drive Third Shot

Let's say your return of serve was weak and short. You see that a fastball is coming your way. What do you do? If the shot is fast and more than about a foot above the net, it will likely fly out of bounds. If it looks like it will stay in bounds, you will need to block the shot. I rarely block shots right back at the issuer or directly at their partner because the opponent team is usually hoping for this. An offensive strategy is to drive the third shot and then poach the blocked shot. So, instead of blocking forward, I angle the block and try to go low to an open space.

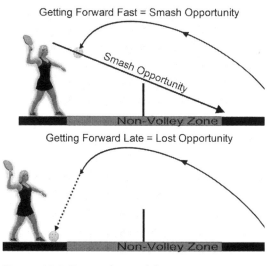

Figure 15-3 Getting forward fast

Now, let's say you are playing a baseline banger who is trying to hit a fastball from the baseline as his or her third shot. If you can execute a block dink (a blocking drop shot), you can almost certainly win the rally with this shot.

Fourth Shot Strategies

Let's say your opponents are trying to hit a third shot drop shot into the kitchen. Here's what to do.

1. Let's say they are successful and their shot bounces in the kitchen where you can't reach it to volley it back. You now have to hit up on the ball from a location near the net. Such a ball location gives no good option for attack. Following such a shot, your opponents should be at or very near the NVZ line, and they should be tightly linked and correctly positioned relative to the ball. In such a case, return the unattackable dink with an unattackable dink.

2. Now let's say that their third shot came over a little high so that, if you reach, you can volley it back. In such a case, volley the shot back to the left heel target, being careful to avoid giving your opponent a volley shot. I call this the "keep them back shot." When you volley their third shot back to the left heel target, you quickly stop their forward progress and give them a difficult shot. So, if your opponents are deep, keep them deep by sending them shots that land near their feet, preferably near the left heel target. Whenever you are fully forward, returning a shot by volleying is better than allowing a bounce. Volleying the ball back takes time away from your opponent, and keeps you from backing up and digging out shots near your feet.

3. Now let's say their third shot came over high, over a foot higher than the net. Now you can put some pace on the ball. Usually the best target is the left heel target of the left opponent.

4. Now let's say the third shot came over really high, allowing a smash put-away. Make sure you hit downward to the left heel target, not giving your opponent a volley shot and not hitting your shot out of bounds.

Fourth Shot Mistakes

1. **Avoid an unforced error.** Most mistakes come from trying to do too much, for example, trying to go too fast, too deep, or too close to a sideline. You should be "ahead in the point" (at an advantage in the rally) with the fourth shot. Remember, the service return team makes the fourth shot and this team should have at least 60/40 scoring odds over the other team. Don't blow it by making an unforced error. Also, don't try to short shot a deep opponent unless you know you have a winner, because you should not invite your opponent forward.

2. **Avoid the volley war.** This is a very, very common error in social play. Here's the situation: you have a volley opportunity for the forth shot and the ball is at or just below the height of the net. You will have to hit up on the ball slightly. A mistake is to start a volley war by giving your opponent a volley shot that can be attacked. A higher percentage action is to hit to the left heel target, giving your opponent a ball that will bounce before he can hit it. Fielding such shots from no man's land is tough. In social play, such shots are usually popped up, allowing a put-away shot.

Pickleball Commandment Number 3: Never Fault on the "Keep Them Back Shot"

Here you are in a very superior position: your team is fully forward with no stress and you have an easy volley opportunity. Your unfortunate opponents are stuck in a very inferior court position. With such an inferior third shot by your opponents, your odds of winning the rally are now greater than 60/40. Faulting on such a forth shot usually has no good excuse.

Making it Happen

In social play, you may not receive many third shot drop attempts from your opponents. Likely, you will receive shots you can volley that should usually lead to winning the rally. Try to track your "conversion success," that is, your ability to cause your opponent to "die in no man's land" (fault before getting forward).

CHAPTER 16: MID-COURT TECHNIQUES AND STRATEGIES

It's called "no man's land," the large region of the court between the baseline and where you stand when at the NVZ line. It's a bad strategic location both for offense and defense. You should not desire to set up there or play from there, especially from deep in no man's land. However, your errors and smart opponents will often force you to play shots from no man's land.

The most frequent reason for getting stuck in no man's land is a poor third shot. Here's the usual scenario. Your third shot drop is fairly good, but it's a tad too high and is volleyed back by opponents who are fully forward. So, your best strategy is to stop, split step, and compress just as your opponent hits the volley, allowing you to dart to either side if necessary. Thus your third shot error (shot was too high) now has you stopped in no man's land. What do you do? Unless the ball is high or you see a hole, the best strategy is to attempt another drop shot into the kitchen. This should give you enough time to get fully forward. Such drop shots from no man's land sound easy, but with your feet exposed, and your opponents targeting them or open spaces, your shots will likely be tough. Thus this trying-to-get-forward period is usually a period of managed emergencies.

This is a common problem among mid-level players. They try to make a third shot drop shot. The shot is too high and it gets volleyed back. Under stress and frustrated with the failure of the first drop shot attempt, they quickly revert to playing "whack and react" against the net team. The usual result is that they "die in no man's land" (i.e., they fault before getting fully forward).

This is a good time to introduce what I call the Most Frequent Mistake in Pickleball: giving a good volley opportunity to an opponent in a superior court position (see Figure 16-1.) This error happens frequently and over and over again in recreational "whack and react" play.

The Most Frequent Mistake in Pickleball
You have both a bad court position and a bad ball position but you decide to hit the ball hard. Now your opponent has both a superior ball and court position.

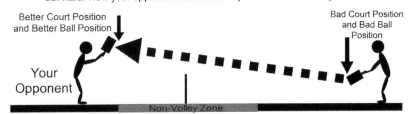

The Smarter Shot
When you are not fully forward, a priority is to get fully forward. So, hit a slow shot that will bounce before your opponent can hit it and quickly move forward.

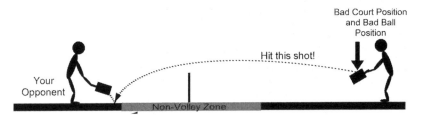

Figure 16-1 The most frequent mistake in pickleball

Here's the rule you need to follow. Whenever you have to hit up on the ball (which is almost always) and when there's no hole in the offense (which is almost always), hit the ball soft enough that it will bounce before your opponent hits it. When in doubt, aim for the left heel target of the left player. If you are not fully forward, use this opportunity to get forward. This shot that bounces gives you time to move and almost assures that your opponent will have to hit up on the ball, thereby limiting aggression. Every time you hit the ball in no man's land, you should advance toward the NVZ line at least a step or two. The softer you hit the ball, the more steps forward you can take.

Coach Mo has a saying: "Your worst shot aimed at the feet or that is low and bounces before being hit will likely be better than your best shot that is higher, giving your opponent a volley opportunity." This advice is more than a cliché or saying. Here's what the data shows. Among equal intermediate or advanced players, even at the 4.5 skill level, in general, when you provide your opponent a volley shot, you will usually lose the rally as a direct result of providing this shot. If, instead, you direct your shot to land at your opponent's feet or to a point where it will bounce in front of him or her, the probability is very low that you will lose the rally as a result of this shot choice. About the only time it makes sense (statistically) to give your opponent a potential volley shot is when an ideal attack setup (e.g., a pop up, short errant lob, or high "floater") allows you to make an attack shot with good power and placement that is unlikely to be returned. Even in this case, an attack shot to the feet is superior to an attack shot that can be volleyed back. Also, as discussed earlier, with the right setup, a third shot drive can be a good choice.

Mid-Court Strategy

Unless the ball is lobbed, the service return team should never get trapped in no man's land. One player is already fully forward. The other returns the serve and runs to the NVZ line before the third shot comes back. So, it's the serving team that usually gets caught there. Here's how to best get through no man's land and up to the NVZ line.

1. Unless the return of serve is short and at your forehand, allowing a drive shot, use the third shot drop.
2. Once you hit the third shot drop, quickly evaluate your shot. The key consideration is to what extent your shot is attackable.

a. If it's high and attackable, get behind the baseline if you can, get in split step, and get low so that you can field a low fastball.

b. If it is low, requiring an upward hit, but can be volleyed, run forward and make as much forward progress as possible, but stop and land in a split step position as soon as your opponent touches the ball. You should be at least seven feet forward of the baseline. From here, unless the ball is high or there is a hole in the offense, attempt to place your shot into the kitchen. If this shot looks like it will drop into the kitchen, run forward and get into split step at the NVZ line. Most good players usually only have to play one shot from no man's land before getting fully forward.

c. If your third shot looks like it will drop into the kitchen, run forward and make as much forward progress as possible, but stop and land in a split step position as soon as your opponent touches the ball. You should be no more than a few feet behind the NVZ line. From here, unless the ball is high or there is a hole in the offense, attempt to place your shot into the kitchen and then get fully up to the line.

3. Being in no man's land when your opponents are fully forward is frustrating. However, unless you have a special opportunity, you should not start a volley war with an opponent who has a superior court position.

Mid-Court (No Man's Land) Techniques

No man's land is the worst place to be caught standing straight up and flat-footed. Most shots will come from a fully forward opponent who is aiming for the left heel target. With the ball issued from such close range, you will not have time to lower or move to return the ball. If you are already compressed, you can likely get any low ball within your reach. Typically, in this location you will be forced to make some of the toughest shots in pickleball, such as a very low volley targeting the kitchen or a half volley targeting the kitchen. If you are compressed and ready for

Mid-Court
(No Man's Land)
Ready Position

A Common Mistake:
Not Following the Cross Court Shot

You make a great cross court drop shot to Point X.
However, instead of following the ball path to point B,
you charge straight forward toward point A. Your partner
correctly charges to point C. Your opponent sees the
broken link and hits between you and your partner.

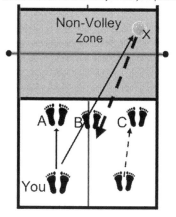

Figure 16-2 Mid-court (no man's land) ready position. You must be lowered, compressed, and ready to field low shots. The paddle should be angled up and should be in a blocking position.

Figure 16-3 A common mistake: not following the cross-court shot

such shots, you improve your chances greatly. Note that when you are trapped in no man's land by volleys coming from an opponent at the net, it's unlikely that you will have time to create a setup. In other words, you may have to hit from the open split step position.

Another key need in this very difficult situation is to stay parallel with and linked to your partner in proper relation to the position of the ball.

Common Mistakes

1. **Charging forward when the third shot is attackable.** Even if you are stopped and in split step, defending against a well placed fastball while in no man's land is almost impossible. You can do a much better job handling these shots from behind the baseline.

2. Getting out of parallel with or disconnected from your partner. Two common mistakes are shown in Figures 16-3 and 16-4. No man's land is dangerous territory. You must stay linked with and parallel (side by side) with your partner.

3. Running up while your opponent returns a shot/failing to stop and split step. No matter how good an athlete you are, when you are running up while a shot from a net man comes heel-deep and out to your side, you will not have time to stop, lower, and reach or change directions to field the shot.

4. Giving up on the kitchen shot. You are stuck in no man's land fielding shots that are difficult. I know that trying to get a shot into the kitchen is difficult and frustrating, but such a strategy, even with the failures included, is a higher percentage strategy than giving up and just sending the net man a volley shot.

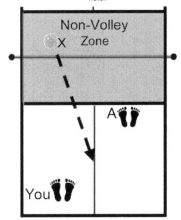

**A Common Mistake:
The Big Hole from Not Being Parallel**

You make a great drop shot straight ahead to point X. You are not sure the shot is good, but your partner does and charges forward. Your opponent hits through the big hole.

Figure 16-4 A common mistake: the big hole from not being parallel

Running Up Error

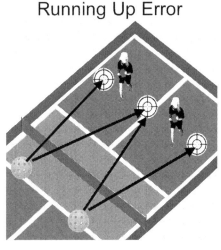

Figure 16-5 Running up error

The above examples are mistakes and also offensive opportunities. So remember to capitalize on your opponents' mid-court mistakes.

CHAPTER 17: SUMMARY OF THE FIRST FOUR SHOTS OF THE GAME

I think it's worthwhile to summarize what we've learned so far. If you and your partner can play the first four or five shots of pickleball strategically and without flubbing, you can likely win most of your games.

The Serve. Aim for the center of the box and provide plenty of clearance over the net. The key need is to avoid faulting. Use a repeatable routine. Line up and aim. Spot the target and visualize the ball flight path. Drop the ball from above and use the paddle stroke to push the ball along the ball flight path. Become resolute that you will follow your routine and not fault on the serve.

The Return of Serve. Just try to get the ball halfway through no man's land. Use a semi-lob if necessary so that you can get fully forward before the third shot comes across the net. If you can, hit the return of serve to whichever opponent is more likely to fault or give you an attackable shot. If your opponents have equal third shot skills, try to hit to the backhand of the even-court player (assuming he is right-handed). Avoid the common mistakes of 1) hitting a flat shot that goes into the net, or 2) hitting a fastball that flies out of bounds deep. The key needs are 1) placing the ball at least halfway back in no man's land without faulting, and 2) getting fully forward alongside your partner before the serving team sends over the third shot. Become resolute that you will avoid aggression with this shot, that you will not fault, and that you will get to the line on time before the third shot arrives.

The Third Shot. This can be tough, but try to hit your shot so that it will bounce before your opponent hits it. If your opponent hangs back, hit the third shot deeper but such that it bounces before being hit. Shots that bounce are not very attackable and provide you more time to scramble forward. If an opponent hangs back or is slow in getting forward, this provides you a generous window for hitting a third shot that will bounce before being hit. If your third shot fails, going too high, try to make a good fifth shot that will bounce before being hit.

The Fourth Shot. If the third shot is great and allows the serving team to get fully forward, the fourth shot is usually a dink. If the serving team fails to get forward, the fourth shot should usually go to the left heel target to keep the team back (the "keep them back shot"). Become resolute that you will not have an unforced error against opponents who are in an inferior court position.

Beyond the Fourth Shot. Once all players are fully forward, dinking the ball is usually the best strategy until a put-away shot presents. When dinking, the key need is to keep the ball in play and unattackable. This takes priority over trying to achieve spectacular placements. Even at the 4.0 skill level, if you can simply hit four or five unattackable dinks in a row, you can likely win the rally.

Suggested Drills for Developing these Shots and Strategies

I am lucky to live in an area where we have a number of 5.0-rated players who compete in the major tournaments such as the U.S. Open and the ASAPA National Tournament. Competitors at this level understand the importance of focused, goal-oriented practice. I am always eager to assist our top players with their drills.

One way to practice is to break down the game into sections and then practice each section. In this way, your game becomes just an extension of your practice. Here are some easy examples of drills for the shots and strategies discussed so far in this book.

Return the Serve and Get to the Line on Time Drill

Only two players are required. Player A makes a normal, diagonal cross-court serve. Player B must return the serve toward the server's side of the court and then get fully forward before the third shot arrives. Player B must ensure that no third shot is allowed to bounce outside the kitchen area. Further, any third shot estimated to bounce in the kitchen within a foot of the NVZ line should be volleyed back to quickly stop the forward progress of the opponent.

Get the Third Shot into the Kitchen under Stress Drill

This drill takes the above drill one step further. Player A makes the serve. Player B returns it back toward the server. Player B also gets fully forward, forcing the server to play the "critical third shot." The server must then try to make a drop shot into the kitchen and scramble forward. The server should attempt to get fully forward following a successful drop shot.

Win the NVZ Line Drill

In this drill, you use one half of the court only, for example, just the right side only. Player A is fully forward at the NVZ line and he stays there. His job is to keep player B from making any forward progress. Player B has the goal of getting fully forward to the NVZ line without faulting. The drill starts with Player B behind the baseline. Player B hits a rather high shot to Player A. This simulates the situation of Player B making a very bad third shot that is attackable. Player A tries to hit shots that cause Player B to fault or not advance. Player B tries to hit shots into the kitchen that help allow forward advancement. To successfully advance, Player B will likely be fielding difficult shots while in no man's land.

CHAPTER 18: DINKING TECHNIQUES AND STRATEGIES

The dinking phase only occurs among players who understand that it's better to postpone aggression and scoring attempts until they are fully forward. These players must also possess skills such as the third shot drop that allow getting forward. Smart players know it's unwise to start a fastball fight with opponents who have a superior court position.

This chapter will not be very relevant to most players. In typical social/recreational play, folks start hitting hard as soon as the ball is served. As a consequence, the ball quickly ends up in the net, out of bounds, or smashed. In recreational play, about two-thirds of rallies end with five or fewer hits (including the serve).

For those folks who wish to play "at-the-line" pickleball, read on.

Suppose all four players are fully forward at the NVZ line. What type of shots do you use now? Typically you use the dink shot. Why use the dink shot? You should dink because you usually have no better options. When all four players are at the line and properly positioned, until the ball gets high or a hole in the offense occurs, the dink is usually the smartest or highest percentage action available. Here's why. When dinking, the ball will only bounce about 16 inches high, which is less than half the height of the net. So, when your opponent hits an unattackable dink to you, you have these choices:

1. **Hit the ball hard.** Here's the problem. If it clears the net, it will likely fly out of bounds. See Figure 18-1. A smart and skilled net player will let such shots fly out of bounds. To be successful with such a shot, the shot needs to hit your opponent or defeat his or her reaction time.

The Body Shot Attack

The "slap shot" attack ball will usually fly out of bounds if you can dodge it.

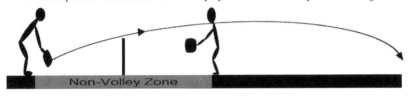

Figure 18-1 The body shot attack

2. **Hit the ball hard, but such that it will stay in bounds.** Here's the problem. You have just given your opponent a great volley opportunity. He now has the ball above the net. To be successful with such a shot, it needs to go through a hole in the offense or defeat reaction time.

3. **Hit an Offensive Lob.** Here's the problem. Unless you have good skill with such shots, or poor lob handling opponents, you will likely lose more points than you will gain from them. Only when you have the combination of a good lobber and a poor lob handler does lobbing result in high percentage play.

4. **Dink the ball.** This is usually the smartest thing to do until somebody pops the ball up.

How to Dink—Footwork

Once you get fully forward, try to keep your toes pinned to the line, (only an inch or two behind the line). If your partner is receiving the serve, go ahead and get both feet pinned in place. You can twist your upper body to watch whether the serve is in or out. Keep a wide stance, feet at least shoulder width apart, as this allows the fastest sideways shuffling. Getting your feet in place early and when you have a chance allows you to avoid looking at your feet when you should be watching the ball.

Avoid stepping back if a ball is headed toward your feet. If you are properly compressed, low, and holding your paddle well in front of your body, you can volley such shots headed toward your feet versus letting them bounce. So, when you have a choice between hitting the ball in the air (volleying) or after the bounce, reach and volley the shot, as fewer bad things can happen if you do. If you let such a ball bounce, it could take an unpredictable bounce or land in a tough spot beside you or behind you. Making a volley shot is easier than digging the ball with a half volley. Also, volleying the ball takes time away from your opponents.

No matter what shot you are hitting in pickleball—a dink, a smash, a volley, a groundstroke—you should seek to hit the ball well out in front of your body. If you let the ball get beside you, you give up angles and your opponent can better predict where your shot will go.

As the ball moves left and right, your team "wall" needs to stay tightly linked, sliding left and right in relation to the position of the ball. Try to preserve your ready position base as much as possible, so use side shuffle steps, if you are able,

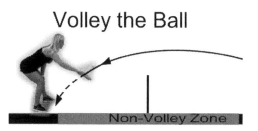

Volley the Ball

Figure 18-2 Volley the ball instead of letting it bounce because fewer bad things can happen.

Contact the ball in front of your body!

Figure 18-3 Contact the ball in front of your body

when moving laterally along the NVZ line. Less mobile players may not possess the speed and agility required for the shuffle step. So, less mobile players may need to use a crossover step, especially to reach wide shots. Crossover steps are not ideal, but they work fine so long as you can keep the ball slow, low, and in the kitchen so that you can uncross and get back in position for the next shot.

Movement along the NVZ line is essential. However, good dinkers stay tight on the NVZ line and don't dance around or move their feet unnecessarily.

To be good at dinking, you must be able to hit the ball when it's very low, barely off the ground. Your opponent will often aim to have the ball land right at your feet. You must be able to hit low volleys and half volleys. Great players bend their knees, meet the ball low, and stay low through contact.

You can use a wall or a practice partner to gain skill at dinking. If you use a wall, try to make the shots rebound so that they come at your feet. Handle these without backing up by making low volleys or half volleys. You will find that you can't do this drill very well unless you are compressed and low.

If you need to step into the kitchen, if possible, do so with one foot only (a lunge) and then push off of it to get re-established behind the line. By the way, if you step into the kitchen, avoid hitting to the near opponent. If you err and get the ball too high, he could hit the ball back to you before you have both feet re-established behind the NVZ line, causing a fault on your part.

When you are involved in dinking, you must stay compressed and low, leaning forward, and on your toes. It helps even more to split step or adjust, if only slightly, each time your opponent touches the ball. You will need the agility, because sharply angled crosscourt dink shots and disguised "misdirection" shots can outrace you if you are not ready. When I am at the line and facing an opponent at the line and I see him standing straight up and flatfooted (therefore, glued in place), I can usually win the rally with just one dink. I use a misdirection shot to place the ball near a sideline.

You must stay linked to your partner, shifting the wall laterally with each lateral shift of the ball position. This can be tiring, but it's necessary. In a crosscourt dinking exchange, the wall should slide back and forth. A savvy opponent will look for a break in the link that creates a hole.

Dinking Ready Position

There are different ready positions depending on your location on the court. Recall that the behind-the-baseline ready position has the paddle perpendicular to the net because you have plenty of time to go to either the forehand or backhand position. The mid-court (no man's land) ready position requires you to be very low and the paddle is typically held in a backhand blocking position. In this region of the court, most shots will be coming very low.

When it comes to dinking, the best ready position depends on your playing ability and your ability to react quickly. Unless you have great skill and reaction time, I recommend a dinking ready position where the paddle is held in a backhand blocking position. Why? If you are fielding a dink, you have plenty of time to switch to either forehand or backhand. If you are fielding an attack shot, you will usually use the backhand. If you are ready in this backhand position, you may be able to punch back the attack shot.

You will see many styles among the top players. Most styles have these common elements:

Figure 18-4 Ready positions

1. The paddle is not hanging down, but is up, out front, and angled up.

2. The players are low and compressed so that they can dart to either side quickly or volley back shots coming toward their feet. If the paddle is angled down, a fastball hitting the paddle will almost certainly go into the net.

How to Dink—Upper Body and Stroke

Though your toes should stay pinned to the line, keep your upper body facing and tracking the ball. Keep your paddle up, out front, and track the ball with it. Make contact with the ball in front of your feet. When at the net in ready position, I do not hold the paddle blade perpendicular to the net. Instead, as my reflexes have slowed, I hold the paddle more parallel to the net, keeping the face about perpendicular to the location of the ball. In this way, the face tracks and points at the ball and I'm always ready to block should a fastball get issued. I prefer to have my left hand touch the edge of the paddle when I am in ready position near the net.

As with all ground strokes, use the "one unit arm," with no elbow or wrist action. As with the volley, the dink stroke is compact with only a small backswing and small follow through. As with the volley, through the whole stroke, the paddle should stay in front of your body. The stroke movement comes from torso rotation and the shoulder, not from the elbow or wrist. The paddle goes from low to high in a nearly linear path with the face staying open and the face angle changing very little during the stroke. Through the strike, think about pushing straight forward and hitting four balls in a row. Watch the ball hit the paddle and keep your head down throughout the stroke. Follow through toward the target.

There are two main ways folks hold the paddle during dinking. I call one way the tennis technique, and the other the shovel technique.

The Tennis Technique

The tennis way is with the paddle parallel to the ground or with the paddle tip slightly upward. Most folks from a tennis or table tennis background prefer this method. It's basically like hitting any other low ground stroke where you keep the paddle head from dipping low. The authors prefer this method and it's more popular with the best players. I think the tennis technique allows you to handle low and high balls and shots requiring reaching better than the shovel technique. The tennis technique also allows you to add backspin, which 1) helps float the ball over the net and 2) helps stop the ball near where it bounces. Players who use this technique must get low and open the paddle face (tilt it upward). When the ball is very low, the paddle may be very open, like a nine iron golf club.

When I make backhand shots, I prefer to use my left hand as a guide for setting the paddle face. If I am in a continuous backhand dinking exchange, I bring the paddle back to my left hand between hits.

Tennis Style Forehand Dink

Key points: 1) The contact point is in front of your body. The paddle is about parallel to the ground and the face is very open. 2) Use the Continental grip and keep the wrist firm. 3) Bend your knees and meet the ball low. 4) Notice the toes are only an inch behind the NVZ line. Try to keep your toes pinned to the line. 5) The stroke comes from the shoulder. The paddle's forward movement goes from low to high. 6) Watch the ball all the way through contact.

Tennis Style Forehand Dink Contact Point

Figure 18-5 Tennis style forehand dink

Tennis Style Backhand Dink

Key points: 1) The contact point is in front of your body. The paddle is about parallel to the ground and the face is very open. 2) Use the Continental grip and keep the wrist firm. 3) Bend your knees and meet the ball low. 4) Notice the toes are only an inch behind the NVZ line. Try to keep your toes pinned to the line. 5) The stroke comes from the shoulder. The paddle's forward movement goes from low to high. 6) Watch the ball all the way through contact.

The Shovel Technique

In this technique, the tip of the paddle points to the ground like the tip of a shovel. Here's how that works. Point your paddle toward the ground at about a 45 degree angle as if pretending to shovel snow toward the net. Remember to make contact with the

Tennis Style Backhand Dink Contact Point

Figure 18-6 Tennis style backhand dink

ball well in front of your feet. When hitting the forehand dink, turn your wrist as far to the right as possible and lock it there. This will keep the face of the paddle straight and facing forward. When hitting the backhand dink, turn your wrist as far to the left as possible and lock it. Again, use the "aim-and-then-hit-four-balls-in-a-row" system. After each hit, return the paddle to the ready position in front of your body.

The shovel technique has about all of the disadvantages discussed in Chapter 3 on paddle holding techniques. Folks who use this technique often introduce wrist action, which adds to shot variability. There are two small advantages of the shovel technique. One is that you use the length of your paddle, not the width, to get under the ball. Another is that you can better disguise sneaky offensive lobs, which can work well at lower levels of play.

Shovel Style Forehand Dink

Contact Point   Follow Through

Figure 18-7 Shovel style forehand dink

Shovel Style Forehand Dink

Key points: 1) The paddle has a very open (upward) face. Aim it and "hit four balls in a row" along the intended ball flight path. 2) The wrist is firm. There should be no wrist or elbow action in dinking shots. 3) The stroke comes from the shoulder. 4) You must bend your knees and lower to get beneath the ball. 5) Watch the ball and don't peek until the ball is gone. 6) It's okay to step into the kitchen, but step in with one foot only and then push off with the same foot to get back behind the NVZ line and in your ready position.

Shovel Style Backhand Dink

Key points: 1) The paddle has a very open (upward) face. Aim it and "hit four balls in a row" along the intended ball flight path. 2) The wrist is

Shovel Style Backhand Dink

Contact Point   Follow Through

Figure 18-8 Shovel style backhand kink

firm. There should be no wrist or elbow action in dinking shots. 3) The stroke comes from the shoulder. 4) You must bend your knees and lower to get beneath the ball. 5) Watch the ball and don't peek until the ball is gone. 6) It's okay to step into the kitchen, but step in with one foot only and then push off with the same foot to get back behind the NVZ line and in your ready position.

Basic Dinking Strategy

Keep the Ball in Play

Your first priority should be to get the ball over the net and keep it in play. You need to allow a generous margin for error. So try to have all of your dink shots clear the net by at least a foot. Dink shots require a rather severe upward hit. Make sure the trajectory is arcing, not flat. So, put an arc on the ball and let gravity drop it into the kitchen. Dink flubs that go into the net account for a large portion of unforced errors, even among top players. Whenever the ball hits your paddle away from the sweet spot, you lose distance and the ball goes into the net. So, again, it's important to allow a generous margin for error. See Figure 18-9. I notice that 5.0-level players dink more conservatively than 4.5-level players, who can't resist attempting flat trajectories and sharp angles. As you get better at dinking, avoid the temptation to increase aggression by hitting

Good and Rather Risky Dink Trajectories

The good trajectory clears the net by a foot and the ball lands close to the net, making it unattackable. The flat and low trajectory has a high rate of faulting due to the ball going into the net.

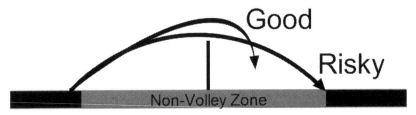

Figure 18-9 Good and rather risky dink trajectories

flatter trajectories that barely clear the net. If, instead of trying to hit a flat trajectory or sharp angle, you simply hit five or six consecutive good, unattackable dinks per Figure 18-9, you will almost certainly win the rally.

I think wall practice is a great way to improve dinking consistency and ball placement skill.

Another thing you need to do to keep the ball in play is communicate with your partner, especially on shots coming between the two of you. Call it early, saying, "mine" or "yours."

Watch Your Opponent's Paddle

As you get into higher-level play, you must watch out for an attack; specifically, you have to look out for the "slap shot" or shot to the body. Such attack shots will almost certainly fly out of bounds if you can dodge them. However, to dodge them successfully, you must detect these shots early, even before your opponent impacts the ball. Even when such shots are disguised, the best players can begin ducking before the ball crosses the net. I've seen this many times by watching slow motion videos: pros who can detect and dodge an "out ball" before the ball crosses the net. How do they do it? They do it by being keenly aware of their opponent's paddle. At the moment they read the acceleration and attack intent, they begin to get out of the way. A good player will also be aware of the height of the contact point (the extent to which the opponent is trying to attack an unattackable ball) and other factors like wind direction. A fastball detect and dodge drill is discussed at the end of this chapter.

Targets and Placement

Place a high percentage of your dink shots down the middle toward the left player's left foot—in other words, low to the backhand for a right-handed player. For most players, low to the backhand will be their weakest shot. Specifically, aim for the left heel target. Not only is a shot to the left heel target tough to return, it's also nearly impossible to do anything offensively with such a shot. Hitting to this spot has other advantages.

135

You are about 10 feet away from both sidelines, thereby avoiding out of bounds risk. You are hitting over the lowest part of the net. You can cause confusion between your opponents regarding who will hit the ball. Many times, neither will hit the ball.

Avoid giving a forehand shot to the player directly opposite you, as this could invite a fastball attack.

Only try sharp crosscourt (post to post) dink shots when you get a ball (receive a shot) that is easy to handle. In general, it's safer to return a shot in the general direction from which it arrived, rather than changing the direction of the ball.

Getting Out of Trouble

Let's say a well-placed sharp crosscourt shot has taken you beyond a sideline. The worst thing to do is pop it up to the near opponent. He will be looking for this put-away opportunity.

There are several ways to handle the situation of being pulled wide. If you can hit the shot back crosscourt and into your opponent's kitchen, this is a great choice as it gives you time to get back into position. But, let's say you cannot make a crosscourt shot. The easiest thing to do is "go with the pitch" and hit the ball straight ahead down the near sideline very softly so that it lands very close to the net. This should slow the game enough to allow you to get back into position. Of course, you should not hit to the near opponent if you cannot regain your court position.

Another choice is an around-the-post shot. In the worst case of trouble, you may have to lob the ball.

Remember, when pulled wide, do not give the near opponent a pop up and do not give the near opponent any shot, not even an unattackable dink, if you cannot regain your court position in the process. Your partner cannot protect the entire court.

Opening a Hole by Working the Point

Once you get good at placing the ball you can start trying to open holes. This usually involves drawing an opponent to a sideline and then hitting down the middle or drawing an opponent to the middle and then hitting toward a sideline. Here are some examples.

If you hit most of your dinks down the middle to the left player's left heel (low to the backhand), the opponent on the right might creep toward the middle and expose his or her backhand territory. Hit to the exposed area. This might open the middle. If the left player slides over to cover the middle, hit to the left of him toward the sideline, in other words, hit "inside-out." Of course leave a margin for error.

Backhand to backhand crosscourt dinking exchanges are common. They are also taxing as the defensive wall must keep moving, sliding back and forth. In particular, a player engaged in the backhand-to-backhand exchange must keep sliding back to the middle after each hit. If the right opponent gets tired, lazy, or bored, he opens a hole in the middle. If the left opponent stops sliding, there may be a hole toward his or her sideline.

Wait to Pull the Trigger

When you have the combination of patience and being able to keep the ball in play, you can usually win the dinking game by waiting for the opponent to either fault or do something dumb (such as choosing a lower percentage option like starting a fastball fight from a low dink bounce). When you know that your team has superior dinking skill, keep dinking and don't start a fastball fight unless you have a high probability winner.

Patience is a virtue when dinking. Wait for a hole or a pop-up before getting aggressive. If the ball comes to you a foot above the net and you can volley the shot, hit it down the middle. If the ball gets popped up higher, hit downward and down the center toward a left heel target. Don't start a fastball fight with just any shot that comes over that you can volley. If the ball is less than a foot above the net, then before it travels seven feet across the NVZ, it will probably drop to the height of the net or below, which creates a low percentage shot if you choose to hit the ball hard.

Also, if your opponent hits a low ball (like a dink bounce) and tries to hit a fastball at you (in other words, if he tries to hit a body shot at you

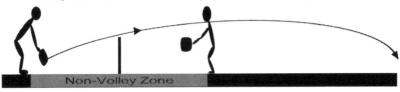

The Body Shot Attack
The "slap shot" attack ball will usually fly out of bounds if you can dodge it.

Non-Volley Zone

Figure 18-10 The body shot attack

from a dink bounce), dodge it if you can and allow the shot to fly out of bounds. See Figure 18-10.

When to Attack

Throughout this book, we emphasize not making errors, "working the point," not trying to place shots near boundary lines, and "giving your opponent a chance to lose." Don't mistake this to mean that you should play defensively only. At lower levels of play, you can usually win by letting your opponents fault. However, at higher levels of play, you cannot win by only playing defensively. When the ball gets high you must attack (usually down the middle to the spot between the left opponent's feet and the right opponent's feet), and when a hole is created, you must go through it (usually "rolling the ball" down the middle). So, against skilled opponents, you cannot forego making attacks when the opportunities are there and waiting. Yes, some attack attempts will backfire. Still, you have to go with the percentages. When an attack is likely to end the rally in your favor, make the attack.

Sadly, many attack attempts are botched. Increasing power decreases control. Most coaches advise not using more than 80 percent of your maximum power on any shot. Coach Mo always advises not hitting the ball any harder than necessary to ensure accuracy and consistency. Coach Mo also advises not using more power than is necessary to effect the put-away. A soft put-away to an open space is usually more effective than a powerful put-away toward a boundary line.

Common Mistakes

1. **Trying to hit a winner rather than trying to keep the ball in play.** Hitting a sharp crosscourt winner brings tremendous joy, but for most players, attempts at such shots cause more lost points than gained points. If you simply commit to hitting unattackable dinks that clear the net by a foot, you will win more dinking battles than by going for aggressive placements. Often, when involved in a crosscourt dinking exchange, an aggressive player tries to go closer and closer to a sideline, eventually going out of bounds wide.

2. **Trying to "kiss the tape."** Developing players, as they get better, often start trying to lower their shots too much, "kissing the tape" at the top of the net. This is not smart, as any slight mis-hit will dump the shot into the net.

3. **Not staying low and compressed.** You may think you can lower in time to return a shot headed toward your feet. You cannot. You must already be compressed. A shot to the feet of a net man who is standing tall is almost certainly a winner.

The Fastball Attack: The Detect and Dodge Drill

Two people are required. One half of the pickleball court only is used. Both players start fully forward at the NVZ line. Player A is the attacker. Player B is the defender/dodger. We begin by dinking. Player B intentionally and continuously dinks to the attacker's forehand, but all such "feed" shots should bounce in the kitchen. At some point after, say, five to ten dinks, the attacker must attack and attempt to make a winning shot. The attacker's goal is to score as a result of the attack. The defender/dodger's goal is also to score. The defender may choose to dodge or hit. After, say, 10 attack attempts, the players can swap roles. Next, add up your attacking and defending scores. After a few tries at this drill, I think you will become much better at detecting and responding to attacks.

Pickleball Commandment Number 4: Never Have an Unforced Error of Hitting Your Dink into the Net or Out of Bounds

In a typical dinking exchange, there is almost no good reason or circumstance beyond your control that should cause your dink to go into the net or out of bounds. In other words, dinks that go into the net or out of bounds are, in most cases, unforced errors. Instead of trying to get low and angled "winner dinks," focus on hitting reliable, unattackable dinks that clear the net and sidelines by wide margins. Keep giving your opponent a chance to fault.

Making it Happen

There is almost no good reason or circumstance beyond your control that should cause your dink to go into the net. In other words, a dink that goes into the net is, in almost every case, an unforced error. On your next outing seek to avoid having any dink go into the net, and keep track of every dink that you hit into the net. So, don't try to "kiss the tape," don't go for crosscourt winners, and don't try to go down the sideline. Instead, seek to continuously hit unattackable dinks that clear the net by a foot. All coaches drill into their students: 1) never miss a serve, and 2) never miss a return of serve. I suggest that you also drill in: you should never hit a dink into the net.

CHAPTER 19: VOLLEY TECHNIQUES

A volley is a shot made before the ball bounces. In other words, it's a ball hit in the air before it bounces in your court. Most often the volley shot is used at the NVZ line, but sometimes it is used from no man's land.

Learn How to Volley Outside of Regular Play

When volleying at the NVZ line, the action is so fast that about all you can do is react. You can't consciously think through the steps or techniques. So, you need to develop the technique and skill outside of regular play using drills so that your volleys work automatically when a fastball fight occurs. This book can teach you some techniques, but you are not going to become good at volleying just by reading a book.

A great way to develop volley skills is with a practice partner. Here is a fun drill. It's like playing beach paddleball. You simply volley the ball back and forth. Initially, you should strive to keep the rally going, perhaps by counting how many hits you can make before faulting. Once you get fairly good at keeping the ball going, speed up the action to get even better and have your partner attempt to give you alternating forehand and backhand shots. As you get better, begin to challenge each other more. Soon you will learn where to place the ball to create difficult returns. You can also develop volley skills using a practice wall. I like to practice hitting alternating forehand and backhand volleys at targets on a practice wall. This greatly improves hand-eye coordination, stroke technique, and ball placement skill. See Figure 19-1.

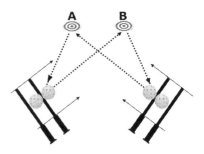

Figure 19-1 Volley drills—alternating forehand and backhand volley shots against a practice wall

Volley Technique

Always be in a ready position with the paddle up and in front of you. Stay fully forward with your toes only an inch behind the NVZ line. When I'm close to the net, in the ready position, I try to keep the paddle face "looking at" and tracking the ball. Keep the paddle head above your wrist. If the paddle face dips low and a fastball hits it, the face can deflect downward, dumping the ball into the net. Of course the paddle must go to the ball location, but it's best if the paddle face can stay above both the wrist and the elbow with the hand leading the face slightly. By staying compressed and by staying fully forward, you can maximize the number of volleys that you can hit with the paddle head above the wrist and elbow.

As with most strokes, try to use the ready-aim-punch sequence, going from ready position, to quickly and directly taking the paddle to the aim point, and then punching straight out. Of course, if the ball is popped up and floating, you should use a swinging put-away shot if you have mastered the swinging volley.

To the extent possible, try to recover to the ready position after each hit. I realize that close range

Figure 19-2 Volley technique

Figure 19-3 Ready, aim, punch

volley action can be too fast to allow much "resetting." In advanced play, you must always assume that the ball is coming back. So, never quit, but be ready. Try to contact the ball well in front of your body. To volley, you will need to place your hand quickly, set the paddle face, and then pop or punch the paddle through the strike. Usually the follow-through is short as you will need to "reload" quickly. There's essentially no paddle swing or wrist action. Instead, the wrist needs to be essentially locked. For a forehand volley, some folks liken the action to giving a "high five," where you pop another's hand. So, the close-range volley usually has a very compact backswing and a punch forward compact stroke. You will often just block back the incoming ball.

Of course if somebody pops the ball up, you will use paddle swing and follow-through as you hit the ball downward. Use only enough power to effect the put-away.

Remember to contact the ball well in front of your body. Doing so opens all of the angles, left and right. If the ball gets close and crowds you, you will struggle just to return it. Worse yet, if the ball gets beside or behind you, your angles are very limited and you will be lucky if your return isn't a fault or weak pop up.

Forehand Volley: Aiming the Paddle

Key points: 1) Rotate the wrist quickly and early to aim the face of the paddle toward the ball and then keep the wrist firm throughout the punch. 2) Elbow is bent, ready to extend out for the punch. 3) The lead shoulder points to the target. 4) The back may bend depending on the height of the contact point. 5) Focus on the ball and anticipate its direction. Keep your head forward but lowered to the height of the ball. 6) The paddle face is aimed and motionless for a split second. It is as vertical as possible,

Forehand Volley Aiming the Paddle

Figure 19-4 Forehand volley: aiming the paddle

Forehand Volley Contact Point

Figure 19-5 Forehand volley contact point

ready to punch forward. 7) The knees bend very low if the contact point is low. 8) The feet are shoulder width apart.

Forehand Volley Contact Point

Key points: 1) Wrist and hand slightly ahead of the paddle face. Contact point is well in front of the body. 2) Elbow straightens to punch the paddle forward. 3) Eyes watch the ball fully through contact. The nose is in line with the contact point. Make a sound at the exact moment of contact. 4) Bend the knees as necessary so that the paddle and head are at the height of the ball. 5) The left hand spots the target and helps with balance.

Forehand Volley Follow Through

Key points: 1) The paddle face punches forward until the elbow is fully extended. 2) The right arm is now straight. You should be able to kiss your bicep. 3) Keep focused on the contact point until the ball is away.

Forehand Volley
Follow Through

Front View
Backhand Volley
Contact Point

Figure 19-6 Forehand volley follow through

Figure 19-7 Front view of backhand volley contact point

Backhand Volley Contact Point

Key points: 1) Keep the wrist and hand slightly ahead of the paddle face. Keep the wrist firm. 2) The elbow will straighten during the forward punch. 3) Watch the ball contact the paddle. 4) The paddle is aimed and motionless for a split second and contact is made in front of your body. Make a sound at the exact moment of contact. Your knuckles should point to the target. 5) Bend the knees as necessary so that the paddle and head are at the height of the ball.

Backhand Punch Volley: Aiming the Paddle

Key points: 1) Set the angle of the paddle motionless toward the ball and target direction. 2) Keep the paddle well out in front of your body. Notice that the elbows are 2/3 straight even before contact is made. 3) Bend the knees to bring your nose down almost to the level of the ball. 4) The feet are shoulder width apart and parallel.

Backhand Punch Volley Aiming the Paddle

Figure 19-8 Backhand punch volley: aiming the paddle

Backhand Punch Volley Contact Point

Figure 19-9 Backhand punch volley contact point

Backhand Punch Volley Contact Point

Key points: 1) Let go with your left hand just before contact. 2) Focus on the contact point until after follow through. Do not lift your chin too soon. 3) Extend the elbow and paddle toward the target. 4) Keep the knuckles of your hitting hand pointing toward your target. Keep a firm wrist and punch the volley. Do not swing at volleys unless you are an advanced player. Make contact well away from you and make a sound at the moment of contact. 5) Follow through by fully extending the elbow without changing the paddle face aim. 6) Get ready for the next shot, which may come very fast.

Avoid Hitting Out Balls, Don't Reach High

Even a long volley exchange lasts only a few hits before control of the ball is completely lost. When the action is fast, shots well below head height will likely fly out of bounds if allowed. Your ego will try to keep you in the battle, looking for a dramatic put-away. However, you will win more games when you can allow out balls to go out. Coach Mo reminds his students that when you hit an out ball, your team now has to win the rally twice.

Volley Strategy

Unless you have a better than even chance of being able to put the ball away or defeat your opponent's reaction time, do not give your opponent a ball in the air (i.e., a volley opportunity). Defeating reaction time means causing a fault or a weak return that can be smashed. My analysis shows that if you start a volley exchange and you fail to win it or defeat your opponent's reaction time with your first volley, then you will likely lose the rally. Especially avoid starting volley exchanges when you have an inferior court position, such as you being in no man's land while your opponent is fully forward. In sum, only start a volley war if you think you can likely win it or force a weak return with your first shot.

When a fast volley shot comes straight at your chest, your gut reaction might be to hit straight back at the other guy's chest. However, your first priority should be to aim downward toward your opponent's feet when possible. If the ball is too low for aiming at the feet, go down the center. Another option is to just block/dink, taking pace off the ball to "reset" the point.

More strategies follow below.

Common Situations & Appropriate Strategies

Let's look at a variety of situations where a volley will or might be used.

Mid-court strategy. Your opponents are both fully forward and you are right in the middle of no man's land. His shot to you comes to your backhand and it's about two feet off the ground. What do you do? The general rule is that whenever you are not fully forward, your first priority is to get fully forward. Trying to win a volley war from mid-court against opponents who are fully forward is a low percentage proposition. So, unless there's a hole in the offense or the ball is high, allowing a smash, usually the best way to get forward is to hit a soft shot that will bounce before your opponent can hit it. So, in this case, use a soft volley that will make your shot bounce in the kitchen. A very important skill in pickleball is being able to "take pace off of the ball," in other words, being able to receive a fastball and send it back as a slow ball that will drop to the ground before your opponent can hit it. You can practice this skill with your practice partner while playing the "beach paddleball" volley exchange drill described earlier.

In the above mid-court case, if the volley was a little higher and at your forehand and a slight hole was present, a drive to the hole might be a great shot. Any return would likely be a weak block that would allow you to make some advancement.

Low volley during dinking. You are engaged in a crosscourt backhand dinking exchange with your opponent. Periodically the ball comes very low, in the air, toward your backhand, and toward your feet. What do you do? This is a very common situation in advanced play. If you are compressed and low, with your knees bent, you should be able to return any low volley. A mistake is to let such shots cause you to retreat or to let such shots automatically trigger aggression. A good choice is to just volley all such very low shots back to the kitchen toward where they came from and continue dinking until a better opportunity arises. When making really low volleys near the net, you will need to angle the paddle face steeply upward, like a nine iron golf club, to ensure your shot goes over the net.

You get attacked with a slap shot (a surprise shot to your torso). All players are fully forward. You dinked the ball and it bounced in front of your opponent, but you've made the mistake of giving your opponent directly opposite you an easy forehand shot. Suddenly the fastball comes right toward your chest. What do you do? The best thing to do, if you can, is dodge the shot. Most "slap shots" made from a dink bounce will fly out of bounds if you can avoid them. But let's say you cannot move. You will need to block the shot. The block shot will likely fail if your wrist is not firm or if the paddle head has dropped or is angled down.

With an unavoidable shot coming at my torso, I always try to block the shot so that it will go between my two opponents. Sometimes you

The Body Shot Attack

The "slap shot" attack ball will usually fly out of bounds if you can dodge it.

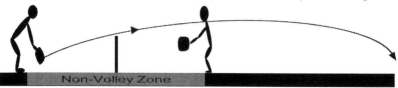

Figure 19-10 The body shot attack

can get a winner from this. If you send a weak block right back at your opponent, you will likely get killed by his or her next shot. By the way, in a volley war, I usually do not try to go directly back and forth with the opponent opposite me, as this becomes a contest of who is stronger and faster. Usually, that person is not me. Instead, I try to hit between the opponents or in such a way that a reach out or paddle flip (e.g., from backhand to forehand, sometimes called jamming the forehand) is required. Also be aware that in a volley war, almost every shot coming your way that would require you to lift your paddle above your chest would likely fly out of bounds if you could dodge it.

A Great Two-Player Drill: Skinny Singles, Starting at the NVZ Line

Here's how to play. You will only use one half of the court. So, imagine that the centerline extends through the kitchen areas. Both players start fully forward. The serve is a dink. After the serve, anything but lobbing is allowed. You can use rally or table tennis scoring if you wish. So, you may dink or choose to start a fastball fight. This game is a great way to learn a bunch of important skills all at once. You learn dinking, dodging, attacking, smart play, and dumb play all in the same game. This drill will also help you learn how to "stay down," make low volleys, and avoid backing away from the line. This is a great game to play while waiting your turn for a regular game of doubles.

Mistakes to Avoid

Just because you receive a shot that can be volleyed doesn't mean you need to attack and give your opponent a volley shot. Suppose you are in the middle of no man's land facing two opponents at the net and you receive a shot at about net height that can be volleyed. In such a case, your court position is inferior compared to the court position of your opponents. Your first priority should be getting fully forward. So, avoid the temptation to blast a shot and instead bump the ball so that it bounces in front of your opponents. Use this opportunity to get fully forward. Remember the Coach Mo saying, "Your worst shot aimed at the feet or that is low and bounces before being hit will likely be better than your best shot that gives your opponent a volley opportunity."

Making it Happen

I don't think you can significantly develop volleying skills in regular game play. I again urge you to find a practice wall, even if the only place is in your bedroom. Remember, you can use a foam or Nerf ball for indoor practice.

CHAPTER 20: THE OVERHEAD SMASH

Introduction

The overhead smash is a hard overhead shot directed downward into the opponents' court, usually as a return of a lob or very high pop-up. The form and stroke action of the overhead smash is very much like a tennis serve. In a way, you can think of a tennis serve as a smash from behind the baseline where the ball must land in the service box. Folks from a tennis background almost always bring a very nice overhead smash technique to their pickleball game.

Forget about the "one unit arm" and firm wrist advice for this shot. To be most effective, this stroke does involve the elbow and wrist. It's not unlike a throwing action or whipping action. To hit an overhead properly and with maximum effect, you need to have full arm extension. So, the contact point must be as high as the center of your paddle with your elbow fully extended. If the ball height is too low to permit this, then make a volley shot.

Vigilance and Fast Reaction

About the only time you will use the overhead smash is to handle a lob that you can reach and that looks like it would land in bounds. Most such lobs will be issued from opponents who are fully forward—in other words, offensive, "surprise" lobs. Being compressed and ready and detecting these lobs early are key needs. You have to watch your opponent's paddle closely. When both teams are fully forward, an offensive lob will travel from your opponent's paddle past your NVZ line in less than one second.

The Footwork

From the ready, open position (ready position facing the net, with your feet about parallel to the net), turn sideways to the net by dropping your right foot back. If necessary, traveling sideways, make a side shuffle step or crossing step to get into position behind the ball. Next, you compress and either leap or step forward into the strike. However, when you are fully forward, a well-disguised offensive lob will usually get past you in less than a second. In such a case, usually all you can do is drop one foot back and leap. When you leap with backward momentum, a scissor kick helps counterbalance the swing and helps you land more safely. There are several YouTube videos that show and explain how to handle lobs and how to execute the scissor kick.

The Stroke

Hopefully you have moved into position behind the ball. You should be sideways to the net. Bring your paddle up behind your head (think of answering the phone with your elbow sticking out), track the ball and point your non-paddle hand at the ball, leap and swing the paddle arm up and forward so that you contact the ball high in the air (think of high-fiving a giant) and in front of your body, about six inches in front of your lead shoulder. The stroke action is like a throwing action. To avoid dropping your chin too soon and taking your eye off the ball, keep watching the contact point until long after the ball is gone. After contacting the ball, follow through by letting your arm continue in a downward arc across your body and toward the ground (think of putting a sword away). Now get back into ready position and assume the ball will come back to you. There are many great YouTube videos that show the technique of the overhead smash.

The Overhead Smash

Figure 20-1 The overhead smash

Photos of the Smash

If you are new to the overhead smash or you are having trouble with the shot, the following photos will show you an easy, basic version of the shot.

The Overhead Smash: Aiming the Paddle

Key points: 1) Keep your wrist firm and motionless for a split second before extending the elbow and snapping your wrist in a whip-like motion. 2) The elbow is bent but will straighten during the strike. 3) The left hand tracks and points to the ball. 4) The eyes watch the ball arrive. 5) The paddle face is slightly open and aimed. 6) The knees are slightly bent. 7) Your weight is on your toes, ready to drive into the ball.

The Overhead Smash Contact Point

Key points: 1) The wrist is moving forward and snapping at the ball. Note that the point of contact is in front of the body. You must get behind the ball. 2) The elbow straightens and extends forward during the strike. 3) Make a sound at the exact moment of contact. 4) The eyes continue to watch the contact point for a moment after the ball is gone. 5) The paddle face is exactly square to the target trajectory. 6) Your weight is on your toes and you are driving into the shot.

The Overhead Smash
Aiming the Paddle

Figure 20-2 The overhead smash: aiming the paddle

The Overhead Smash
Contact Point

The Overhead Smash
Follow Through

*Figure 20-3 The overhead
smash contact point*

*Figure 20-4 The overhead
smash follow through*

The Overhead Smash Follow Through
Key points: 1) The wrist has snapped forward toward the target. 2) The elbow is extended fully forward. 3) The eyes are still directed at the point where contact was made. It's important to "not peek" before hitting the ball.

Basic Placement and Strategy

When you are forward and both opponents are back and parallel, hit between them but not too close to the baseline. When you are at the line ready to smash and both opponents are far back, another option is a fake smash. It starts out looking like a smash, but ends up being an overhead dink.

When you are forward and one opponent is up and the other is back, hit the ball to the closest player's inside foot.

Everybody loves to make a smash winning shot. However, incoming shots anywhere near the center area should be given to the forehand player. So, for two right-handed teammates, allow the forehand (odd court) player to make the smash. Make sure you call him over early, saying, "You take it."

Angled smashes are nearly impossible to return but these shots require skill. Unskilled players often hit such shots too hard and too wide such that they go out of bounds. When you have a nice angle available, a controlled but much slower smash can still be a winner.

Defending Against a Smash

A smash is coming. Where should you be? Most coaches agree that you should avoid being in no man's land when facing a smasher. So, the advice is usually to get either fully forward (up to the NVZ line) or get fully back behind the baseline. Another consideration is that you may not have much time to move. The general rules are as follows.

1. If the smash is coming from deep in the court anywhere near the baseline, then get fully forward, with your paddle up and ready to block. This advice may seem strange. However, with 25 feet of separation between you (at the NVZ line) and your opponent (near the baseline), you should be able to react and field the smash. So, if you make a great defensive lob that goes rather deep but will be smashed back, use the opportunity to get forward.

2. If the smash is coming from the middle of no man's land, if you are back, stay back, get behind the baseline, get lowered and ready, and split step at the moment of your opponent's impact. However, if the smash is coming from the middle of no man's land, and you are forward, get fully forward up to the NVZ line, and get ready with your paddle up. Your goal will be to block the shot back low. With this approximately 20-foot separation, fielding the shot will be a challenge.

3. If the smasher is fully forward and you are fully forward, for example, when you've made a terrible offensive lob, you've got a big problem and there's no good solution. Fit and fast players may be able to get back a little and hope to make a block. If there's no

time to move, get your paddle set to block and hope for a miracle. If the smasher is fully forward and you are back, for example, when you've made a weak defensive lob, stay back, get behind the baseline, get lowered and ready, and split step at the moment of your opponent's impact.

Drills

Of course, you can practice the overhead smash using a practice partner. You can also practice with a tall wall, such as in a gymnasium. You do this by hitting the ball upward and high on the wall to provide a nice high smash opportunity. You can also practice by trying to execute tennis type overhead serves on an empty court. These are all good drills but they do not help develop vigilance and fast response, which are critical.

Lobbing and Smashing Drill

In my opinion, the best way to practice both offensive lobbing and smashing is with a simple one-on-one game that simulates the typical real-life at the line situation. You use one half of the pickleball court only. So visualize that the court centerline extends through the kitchen. Both players start fully forward and the serve is a dink. Player A will be practicing offensive lobs. Player B will be responding to the lob. Once dinking begins, Player A, when ready, must issue an offensive lob over Player B. Player A should attempt to disguise the lob and get it past Player B without the lob getting smashed back. So, Player A has the goal of having his lob lead directly to a win of the rally. If he is successful, he gets a point. However, if his lob goes out of bounds or gets smashed back so that his lob leads directly to a loss of the rally, Player A loses a point. Only Player A wins or loses points. Player B has the goal of keeping Player A from winning any points as a direct result of the lob. If it is unclear whether the lob led directly to a win or loss of the rally, replay the rally. Player A is allowed 10 lob attempts. Dinking mistakes do not count toward points, only lob outcomes. After Player A has had 10 lob attempts, the two players switch roles. After each player has had 10 lob tries, the scores are compared.

With this drill, I think you will dramatically improve your vigilance and response capabilities. In fact, most players in reasonable physical shape can develop their response capability to the point where they can smash any lob except those that land within a foot or so of the baseline.

The Low Overhead Smash

The overhead smash has tremendous power. So, many players use the overhead hitting technique even when the ball is not so high. They do this by lowering their body, usually getting down on one knee. The technique is like the regular overhead smash. Again, the purpose is to bring the power of the overhead to shots that are too low for executing the overhead while standing tall.

Figure 20-5 The low overhead smash

Mistakes to Avoid

1. **Not getting behind the ball.** It can be tough to get behind the ball, especially when dealing with a well disguised offensive lob. However, if you fail to get behind the ball, you will not have power or directional control. Instead, your weak shot might give your opponent an opportunity.

2. **Botching the shot into the net or out of bounds.** Most coaches advise not using more than 80 percent of your power on any shot. Weird and totally unpredictable things happen both in golf and in pickleball when you try to use maximum power. If you back off on the power, you can likely focus on getting the ball started on the right target line.

3. **Taking your eye off the ball and dropping your chin too soon.**
   You need to watch the ball make contact and not drop your chin until after the ball is gone.

Making it Happen

On your next outing, resolve to keep all smashes in bounds and in play.

CHAPTER 21: THE LOB

The lob is a high lofted shot intended to send the ball over the heads of your opponents and deep into the court. Lobs are usually either defensive—issued from deep in the court—or offensive—issued from the NVZ line. The lob shot generates a lot of controversy, arguing, and frustration. I know one thing: I can't stand playing with a partner who keeps trying to lob even though his or her lobs are getting smashed back or are floating out of bounds. Likewise I know some good lobbers who frustrate and anger their opponents.

When you have a great lob, it's a great weapon against an opponent with poor mobility or an opponent who is a poor lob handler, such as an opponent with a weak overhead smash. The lob is usually a low percentage shot against highly athletic players who know how to detect, react to, and handle lobs. A lob does not have to be a winner to be worthwhile. Its main use is to move your opponents away from the net and back toward the baseline.

Lobs are used either defensively, usually as a means of getting out of trouble, or offensively, usually to either get out of trouble or to surprise an opponent.

The Defensive Lob

Let's look at some circumstances where defensive lobs can be useful.

1. Let's say your opponent returned the serve very deep and very fast to a corner. This creates a very tough circumstance for hitting a third shot drop or a successful fastball. If you can get a defensive lob to land, say, six feet or deeper behind the NVZ line, you've got a good chance of getting back in the point. If the lob goes very deep, you've switched from being in a terrible position to being in the dominant position.

2. Let's say your opponent surprised you with a lob and it got past you so that you are going to have to play it after the bounce. You are now several feet behind the baseline and still not stabilized. Again, this creates a very tough circumstance for hitting a third shot drop or a successful fastball. If you can get a defensive lob to land, say, six feet or deeper behind the NVZ line, you've got a good chance of getting back in the point.

I think it's unwise to use a lob as a third shot to avoid learning how to execute a third shot drop. Of the many matches I've analyzed, I rarely see a net positive result of using a lob as a third shot.

Great tennis players seldom lob, but they know how to do it when trouble creates no better option. In the same way, pickleball players at all levels need to practice lobs so that they have an option when there are no other options. I have worked hard to perfect a defensive topspin lob. I only use it when I get in trouble but I've been delighted with the results. When making a defensive lob, try to have the lob go just left of center, over the left opponent's left shoulder. This way, even if the lob is short, you will get a weaker backhand smash instead of a forehand smash.

Defensive Lob Practice and Technique

Defensive lobs are easy to practice with a partner. You simply lob the ball back and forth, trying to get the shot to land about 4–7 feet inside the baseline (to provide a margin for error). Most players make the mistake of hitting these shots too horizontally so that they go out of bounds deep.

It's safer to hit these shots very vertically and very high (especially when playing outdoors), and let them "die high" and fall straight down. Also practice adding topspin to these defensive lobs. If you manage to perfect such a shot, it's a great asset.

The Offensive Lob

The offensive lob refers to an unexpected lob from the NVZ line over your opponent who is at or approaching the NVZ line. This shot works well against opponents with low mobility, opponents not skilled in readiness, and opponents who have weak overhead smashes. A key need against an advanced player is disguise in order to shorten his or her time to react. So, you need to make the lob stroke look like a dink stroke for as long as possible. This is something you can practice using a wall. The other key need is a strategic lob direction to make the lob less reachable, especially by the opponent's forehand. An ideal lob path is down the middle over the left (odd court) opponent's left shoulder, assuming the left opponent is right-handed. This lob often causes confusion between your opponents and it is tough to handle by either opponent. If the left opponent gets the lob, he will be making a rather weak backhand overhead smash instead of a forehand smash.

The Disguised Offensive Lob

Looks like it's going to be a dink...   but suddenly it's a lob.

Figure 21-1 The disguised offensive lob

Offensive Lob Practice and Technique

Lob shots require precision. If it's too short, it gets smashed back. If it's too deep, it goes out of bounds. The "window" for a good lob is rather small. Against really good players, there is almost no window at all, as any lob they can't get to and smash is likely out of bounds.

To consistently get good lobs, you must groove in a good technique. A tall practice wall can be a big help. If you are seven feet away from the wall at an imaginary NVZ line, you aim for a target about ten feet high on the wall. You may be able to stand on a chair or ladder and place a piece of painter's tape on the wall to mark the target. Most lobs are offensive lobs issued from the NVZ line and from a rather low dink bounce. So, when practicing, start dinking and, without stopping, execute the offensive lob, trying to hit the target. The easiest setup is when the ball comes straight across the net to you, not from an angle. This also creates the best situation for adding disguise. Whether you dink or lob, you will scoop the ball from beneath, and whether you dink or lob, the paddle face will have a very upward angle.

A Great Lob Path

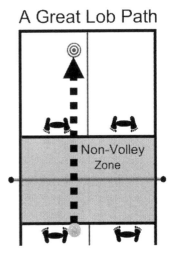

Figure 21-2 A great lob path

It is surprising how steep (how upward) the shot needs to be. From a dink bounce in the kitchen, the angle between your paddle face and a vertical line is less than 45 degrees. Most players who do not practice lobs hit their offensive lobs too horizontally, with many shots landing out of bounds. So, you will set your paddle almost facing the ground. As you bring the paddle to meet the ball, "hit four balls in a row" and follow through, taking the paddle high along the trajectory path. You will need to work into muscle memory the angle and paddle speed required for success. With the wall, you can simulate the real game situation: dink, dink, dink, and then, with minimal changes, issue the surprise lob. Do this exercise over and over to groove the motion and feeling into muscle memory.

A good golfer cannot stop practicing. If they do, they quickly lose their "touch," especially for short shots around the green. In the same way, to keep your touch, you have to practice those shots that require extreme touch, like the third shot drop and the lob.

The Lobbing and Smashing Drill described in Chapter 20 is also a great drill. This drill does a good job of showing you how narrow the window of success really is.

Other Considerations

Wind direction and the location of the sun are considerations when lobbing. Avoid lobbing during gusty winds. A steady and light wind in your face sets up great lobbing conditions as the wind blunts the trajectory, tending to keep the ball in bounds. When the wind is at your back, lobbing is risky. Adding topspin could help, but that is risky too.

It is difficult fielding lobs with the sun in your face. In a competition, you could use this to your advantage when the sun is at your back. By the way, in a tournament, do not let your opponent hear you say that you got blinded by the sun at a certain spot on the court because it will entice him to repeat the shot many times.

In social play, when the sun is a problem, we often agree to suspend offensive lobbing. If you are stuck in a situation of fielding lobs with the sun in your face you may have to ask your partner for help, try to use your other hand to block the sun, or let the ball bounce before hitting it.

Practice before the game. Most folks warm up practicing dinks and third shot drops. You should add lobs to the pre-game warm up to gage wind effects and to get your touch calibrated.

Lob Chasing Basics

From the ready, open position (ready position facing the net, with your feet about parallel to the net), turn sideways to the net by dropping your right foot back. If necessary, traveling sideways, make a shuffle step or crossing step to get into position behind the ball. Next, compress and either leap or step forward into the overhead strike. However, when you are fully forward, a well-disguised offensive lob will usually get past you in less than a second. In such a case, usually all you can do is drop one foot back and leap. When you leap with backward momentum, a scissor kick helps counterbalance the swing and helps you land more safely. There are several YouTube videos that show and explain how to handle lobs and how to execute the scissor kick. In the worst case of a lob that has passed you, you will have to turn and run to get it.

Trying to run straight backwards (backpedaling) is usually difficult and dangerous.

Defending Against the Defensive Lob

With the defensive lob issued from deep in your opponent's court, you should have plenty of time to react, travel, and get behind the ball. Here's a place where communication and teamwork are vital. One teammate should call, "I've got it." The other should read the trajectory and report, "It's in," "no," or "bounce it." If the ball could land out of bounds, allow it to bounce. If the lob appears certain to land in bounds, make every effort to smash the shot, versus letting it bounce, even if you are deep in the court. If you are facing continuous third shot lobs, hang back a few steps behind the NVZ line until you can surmise whether a lob is coming.

Defending Against the Offensive Lob

The best defense against an offensive lob is early detection and immediate reaction. By keenly watching your opponent's paddle, you should be able to "read" what's going to happen before it does happen. The Lobbing and Smashing Drill described in Chapter 20 can help you develop early detection and reaction skills. It is nearly impossible for an opponent to successfully get a good (in bounds) lob past you untouched if you detect and react to the lob quickly. The better you get, the smaller the window of success becomes for your opponent. Among most top players, there is no window and that's why lobbing mostly disappears among the 5.0-rated players.

Now let's say a well disguised lob goes straight over your head. What do you do? If you are a fast player, you need to turn, run, and get the lob. If you get driven deep behind the baseline by the lob, your best shot may be a defensive lob over the left player's left shoulder. Most pros and 5.0-rated players get their lobs instead of expecting help from their partners.

Now let's say a well disguised lob goes straight over your head and you are not a 5.0-rated player but an average senior citizen with many extra pounds and bad knees (like me). What do you do? In general, in the advanced-intermediate arena, if the ball is lobbed straight over your head, then your partner should yell, "I've got it, switch," and he should run back at an angle to retrieve the lob. Anytime you see your teammate in such trouble and you've got a better chance with a shot than he does, call it and take it.

As with the defensive lob, the offensive lob creates a situation where communication and teamwork are vital. If the lob goes over your head and you are able to get it, yell, "I've got it." If you are fielding the lob, your teammate should read the trajectory and report, "no," "it's good," or "bounce it" as appropriate.

What do you do if, in a game situation, your opponents are killing you with successful lobs? Usually only one opponent is doing the damage and usually he is doing it only with a backhand or forehand (but not both), and he is usually only doing it from an easy setup. So, if you can't avoid hitting to the lobber, hit it where he does not have the easy setup. If your opponent is relentless with great offensive lobs, play at the NVZ line until they take their eyes off of you to watch the ball and then quickly drop back a couple of steps to hit an overhead. Of course, it is helpful to choose a highly mobile partner who can get your lobs when you cannot.

Other Comments about Lobs

One of my hobbies is watching and analyzing videos of pickleball matches. I attend and record pickleball matches and then load the videos onto my computer, which has video editing software. Next, I break each match into the individual rallies. I watch the rally in slow motion to analyze shots and their outcomes—both the successful shots and the shots that lead to failure. From this, I compile statistics and try to draw conclusions about what works and what does not. Specifically, I try to determine what things add to the chances of success and what things diminish chances of success.

With respect to lobs, my conclusion in brief is as follows: most players, regardless of level, would be better off not lobbing, except when there are no other options. Here's why.

In the social/recreational arena, on the positive side, the lob handing skill is low. Lobs that get past a player and land in bounds are usually winners. In this arena, most folks do not chase down and return lobs that have slipped past them. However, on the negative side, the folks lobbing usually have poor lobbing skill and a high failure rate, with lobs either being too short and getting smashed or being too long and going out of bounds. My overall finding for social players is that lobs more often lose rallies than win them. However, when a well-practiced good lobber plays among average social players, the good lobber will win more points than he loses. This is a rather rare situation, but I know several folks who have bona fide winning records when lobbing in the social arena. Even at a tournament, I saw a doubles team of expert lobbers use lobbing as their main weapon. They went far along in the brackets before losing. I'm sure that in a social arena, their lobbing would be devastating.

At the professional level, on the positive side, lobbing skill is high, as these folks perform drills, etc. Compared to social players, the pros less often hit their lobs too deep or pop them up too short. However, on the negative side, the players are great lob handlers, rarely letting a good lob go untouched. They can usually smash the lob or otherwise manage to keep the ball in play. As a consequence, among the pros, lobs lead to more losses than gains and thus lobbing frequency is low.

So, among typical social players and among typical professional players, lobs usually lead to more rallies lost than won.

In Sum, When to Lob

Learn how to lob and practice it often. It's a great shot to have when you get in trouble. If you develop a great offensive lob and practice it, it will be a great weapon when playing low mobility players and players who cannot smash the ball. Most players, whether beginner or advanced, will be better off not lobbing except when in extreme trouble. Most folks at all levels underestimate their error rate and the effect it has on the outcome of the game.

CHAPTER 22: THE DROP VOLLEY (THE DROP SHOT)

In this chapter, we discuss the drop shot. Here, we are not talking about the third shot drop described in Chapter 14. The third shot drop is usually issued from deep in the court, and it's not a volley shot. The drop shot described in this chapter is a soft, short volley shot with backspin issued from the NVZ line designed to drop over the net and into the kitchen.

What is the Drop Volley Shot?

The drop shot is a softly hit shot with backspin that falls into the opponent kitchen just after clearing the net. In some ways, it's like a dink with backspin. This shot requires skill and touch in order to create reliable winners.

When to Use It

This is a great shot to use against opponents with low mobility, opponents who like to play deep, and opponents who have retreated to the baseline, for example, to field a lob shot.

An important point is that the drop shot should only be used with the intent to achieve an outright winner, because otherwise it's a mistake to enable your opponent to come forward. Remember, when your opponent is deep, keep him or her deep. Never enable an opponent to advance forward. Therefore, be careful when using drop shots against highly mobile opponents.

Here are some great circumstances for using the drop shot.

- **After a lob.** Let's say you hit a great lob that takes your opponents all the way to the baseline. Your opponents hit you a shot that you can volley. This is a great situation for hitting a soft drop shot toward the post of the deep player.

- **Your opponents are backing up.** Let's say your opponents popped the ball up and now they are backing up to the baseline expecting a fast hit. Rather than hitting the ball hard, you could likely get a winner from a drop shot.

- **Bangers who stay back.** Many players from a singles tennis background like to issue fastballs from deep in the court. Once you develop the touch, you could likely get a winner from a drop shot.

- **High third shot from deep.** Let's say your return of serve was deep, putting your opponent behind the baseline. He tries to make the third shot drop, but the shot comes to you high. Under this circumstance, he's afraid to charge forward. Of course you could volley this shot back to the left heel target. However, with this much separation, a good drop shot toward a post should be a winner.

The Technique

Use the Continental grip (see Chapter 3). Your bottom two fingers (pinky and ring finger) should grip the paddle normally; your other three fingers should grip just tight enough to prevent the paddle from twisting during contact with the ball. So, overall, you are trying to use a softer than normal grip to better enable absorbing the impact, thereby taking pace off the ball.

To the extent possible, turn your shoulders in preparation for the stroke. Point your front shoulder toward the target. Do not let the head of the paddle drop below the wrist. Bend your knees as necessary to meet the ball and allow a level push-forward stroke. Follow through by pushing the paddle forward along the target line.

Keep the paddle face open (facing upward) throughout the stroke. You must stroke the ball, not chop at it. The stroke goes from high to lower to leveling out in the shape of a quarter moon. See Figure 22-1. Ready your paddle about one foot above where you plan to contact the ball, which should be in front of your body. As you contact the ball, the paddle brushes the ball, putting backspin on it. As you slide your paddle under the ball, it's like turning a key. The imparted backspin helps stop the ball from moving forward after its bounce. The follow-through is compact and the paddle face is very open, nearly parallel to the ground at the conclusion of the stroke. This shot requires a very soft touch. Some coaches advise to imagine "catching the ball" on the face of the paddle at the point of contact.

Figure 22-1 Drop volley paddle path

This stroke does involve straightening the elbow, so it is not a "one unit arm" shot. At the conclusion of the stroke, your elbow should be completely straight.

As with all shots (except a few mis-direction shots), watch the ball through contact, not lifting your head until after you complete the entire stroke. As Coach Mo says, "sound like a pro," and make a sound at the moment of impact as a means to ensure that you are watching the ball all the way to the paddle and not lifting your head too quickly.

Don't try to get a trajectory that just barely gets the ball over the net. Along with the risk of faulting into the net, such a flat trajectory sends the ball deeper into the court than a slight pop-up trajectory, which better clears the net and stops shorter.

Most drop volleys are placed crosscourt near the post on the side of the court farthest away from an opponent.

This shot requires much technique and touch. All shots requiring "touch" have to be frequently practiced.

Photo Sequences of the Drop Volley

The drop volley described is essentially the same as the drop volley used in tennis. There are many great You-Tube videos that show the drop shot both for tennis and pickleball. The photo sequences below illustrate some key points.

Forehand Drop Volley

Figure 22-2 Forehand drop volley

Backhand Drop Volley

Figure 22-3 Backhand drop volley

The Forehand Drop Volley

Key points: 1) The paddle starts high, then slices under the ball, and then ends facing very upward. 2) The lead shoulder points toward the target. 3) The elbow is bent when aiming but it straightens through the stroke. 4) The eyes watch the ball all the way to the contact point. Keep the eyes on the contact point until the ball is gone. 5) Especially with this shot, you must bend your knees and lower your body to allow you to have the paddle level at impact. 6) Follow through by pushing the paddle forward along the target line.

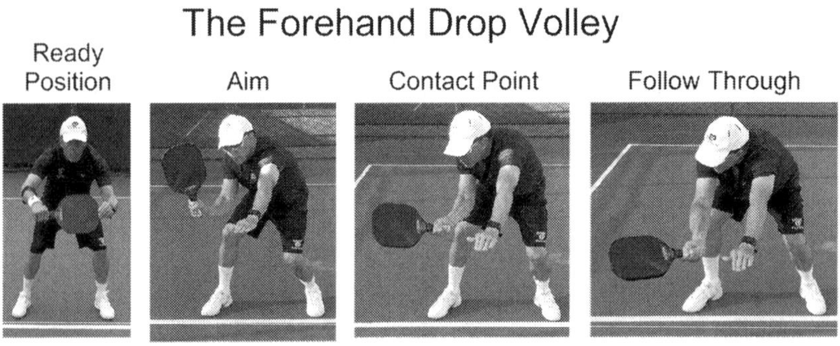

The Forehand Drop Volley

| Ready Position | Aim | Contact Point | Follow Through |

Figure 22-4 The forehand drop volley

The Backhand Drop Volley

Key points: 1) The paddle slices under the ball, and then ends facing very upward. 2) The elbow straightens through the stroke. 3) The eyes watch the ball all the way to the contact point. Keep the eyes on the contact point until the ball is gone. 4) Especially with this shot, you must bend your knees and lower your body to allow you to have the paddle level at impact. 5) As the right arm moves forward, the left arm moves backwards to maintain balance.

The Backhand Drop Volley

| Ready Position | Aim | Contact Point | Follow Through |

Figure 22-5 The backhand drop volley

What if the Shot Gets Returned?

Let's say your opponent was faster than you anticipated. He got the drop shot and smartly dinked it back. What do you do?

If his momentum carried him into the kitchen, hit a soft shot (one that is sure to land in bounds) right at his torso, forcing him to hit before getting re-established behind the NVZ line, thus creating an opponent fault.

If he stayed out of the kitchen but he's still not collected and ready, lob over his backhand shoulder.

Avoid the Big Mistake

The big mistake is trying to put too much backspin on the ball by chopping or hacking in a downward fashion. Indeed, chopping imparts a lot of spin, but it also increases the shot failure rate.

The Block Dink Drop Shot

The classic drop shot just discussed takes skill to master. Any time you brush the ball to impart spin, the difficulty of the shot increases as you must match the timing of the moving paddle and the moving ball. This becomes very difficult if the incoming shot is fast.

The block dink is a good way to make a drop shot with an incoming fastball. I like to use two hands if possible. This keeps the fastball from deflecting the paddle if the ball hits the paddle off center. The paddle face must be open (opened upward), no matter how fast the incoming ball is traveling. There's not much stroke involved, just a block. Try to direct the shot crosscourt and away from the nearest opponent.

The Block Dink Drop Shot

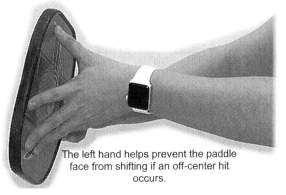

The left hand helps prevent the paddle face from shifting if an off-center hit occurs.

Figure 22-6 The block dink drop shot

Drills to Develop the Technique

1. To some extent, you can develop the shot using a practice wall. Hit a hard shot at the wall and then use a drop shot to handle the rebound.
2. Another drill used to develop the "soft hands and touch" involves trying to catch the ball on the paddle. The coach or practice partner feeds the ball from the baseline and the player, using soft hands, tries to catch the ball on his or her paddle, with just one bounce off the face of the paddle. This soft touch is similar to bunting a baseball. As skill develops, the coach increases the speed of the feeds.

3. Have a practice partner hit shots to you from deep in the court. Your goal is to make a soft drop volley that lands in the kitchen. Increase the feed speed as skill develops.

Making it Happen

The drop shot is a shot you should learn. On your next outing, use it when you get a volley opportunity and see that both of your opponents are deep.

CHAPTER 23: MISCELLANEOUS STRATEGY TIPS

Introduction

As we have covered the serve, the return of serve, the third shot, the "keep them back" shots, and dinks, we have talked about shot goals and strategies. This chapter is devoted to talking about the more general strategies of pickleball.

Weakest Player's Weakest Shot

Make the weakest opponent play his or her weakest shot. All social/recreational players know to hit the ball to the weak opponent. They might say something to their partner like, "Keep hitting it to Fred. He can't get two shots in a row back." But, most social/recreational players stop there. You need to go the next step and make the weak player play his or her weakest shot. Usually this is a shot to the left heel target. Remember, the left heel target is not the left heel, but the open space out to the side of the left heel. Be relentless in making your opponent scrape up and dig out difficult low-to-the-backhand shots.

Dealing with Handedness

To give yourself the best chance of winning, you need to be aware of opponent handedness and how to best deal with the handedness situation. Unless otherwise noted, the targets described in this book assume that your opponents are right-handed. For example, the "low-to-the-backhand left heel target" assumes that the opponent is right-handed.

Let's look at a common situation: both opponent backhands are in the middle (the odd court opponent is left-handed). When your opponents have both backhands in the middle, it's a good situation for your team and a bad one for their team. As both opponents must reach across their body to cover the middle, they must stay very tightly linked to protect against the down-the-middle shot. They will also be protecting this vital zone with backhands, which are usually weaker than forehands. So, when facing such an opponent team, keep your shots to the middle and look for a hole in the defensive wall.

It's also rather easy to lob against such opponents—just send the lob right down the middle. Either person trying to hit it will be using a backhand. In tournament play, stacking is used to keep the left-handed player on the even court, thereby allowing both forehands to be in the middle.

Patience, Playing Steady, and Giving Your Opponent a Chance to Lose

The hallmarks of lower-level play include quickness to aggression; rather careless issuing of shots that can be volleyed back, especially to opponents who have a better court position; attempts to hit difficult shots (such as lobs and slap shots); attempts to hit difficult targets (such as down the line or crosscourt toward the sidelines); and, of course, flubs and mis-hits. Better players bide their time, continuously issuing safe, unattackable shots, while waiting for the put-away opportunity. Better players often never get the put-away opportunity when playing less competent players because the less competent players, given two or three shots, will self-destruct.

The above is not just opinion, but comes from the statistics of hundreds of tournaments. Analysis of many tournament videos of 3.0–3.5-rated players yields the following (sobering) statistics:

- About half of the rallies end with only four or fewer shots taken. I realize this sounds unbelievable. So, after the serve and return of serve, about half of rallies end with only two additional hits made.

- About two-thirds of rallies end with five or fewer hits.
- Almost all rallies end due to player unforced errors and mistakes (e.g., shot flubbed into the net, shot goes out of bounds, low ball popped up followed by put away).

Again, at this level of play, almost every shot is either an error or a poor choice, the most frequent being providing your opponent an easy volley shot instead of an unattackable shot that bounces.

So, at this level of play, if you give your opponent two or three unattackable shots, your opponent will very likely lose through his or her own faults. When an advanced player is paired with, say, a 3.5-rated player, the advanced player's advice to his or her partner is, "Please just keep the ball low and in play and give the other team a chance to lose."

Most players think that winners win by hitting winners and that the key to winning is to try to hit more winners. This is incorrect; usually the opposite is true. Game outcome is usually tied to unforced errors. Even at the top pro level, there are, on average, 17 unforced errors per game. The number of unforced errors is, on average, three times higher than the number of winners. In a typical game to 11 points, a third of the points will come from opponent unforced errors.

So, even at the highest level of play, you have to think in terms of not faulting as a key strategy.

Poaching

A poach is when you cut in front of your partner, take his or her shot, and volley it back to your opponent. The element of surprise is key. Here are some strategies.

Poach the third. Consider this scenario. Your teammate is returning the serve from the even court, while you are fully forward. He never gets fully forward on time, so your opponents keep sending their third shots through the open net position. You are fuming because your opponents are getting away with murder, basically getting a free ride to the net. Here's how to conduct the poach. The moment your opponent commits to hitting his or her shot to your sluggish teammate, dart over and smash it down the middle.

Fake a poach of the third. Consider this scenario. Your teammate is returning the serve from the even court, while you are fully forward. Because he never gets fully forward on time, your opponents keep sending their third shots through the open net position. Here's how to perform a fake poach. Just before your opponent commits to hitting his or her shot, push off of your left foot and spring over a short step to the right, but then spring off of your right to get back where you were. Make sure you do this a moment before your opponent hits, giving him a chance to hit to you. Often the fake poach will draw the shot to you. Poaching and faking a poach will make your opponent start sending their shots out of bounds wide to avoid the poacher.

Avoid Low Percentage "Sucker Shots"

Most books on doubles tennis strategy will advise against these two sucker shots.

Down the line from deep in the court. People think they have better capability in hitting a target than they do. If you are at your baseline, a paddle face error of only five degrees translates into being laterally off target by about four feet at your opponent's end of the court. Rarely do you see a pro try the down-the-line sucker shot. Even at the 4.5 skill level, this shot will lose more points than it earns. The only time to try this shot is when the hole is huge and the opponent near it is weak.

Shots diagonally toward a sideline from deep in the court. It's okay to hit soft shots like dinks and drop shots crosscourt. However, trying to place a shot near a sideline when you are hitting from deep in the court is a low percentage act. Rarely do you see a pro hit any shot out of bounds wide.

Outdoor Play Considerations: Wind and Sun

Wind speed and direction and the location of the sun can be big factors in outdoor play, especially when lobbing. When playing outdoors, there is almost always some wind, even if you can't feel it. For example, in Richmond, Virginia, the wind speed averages about seven miles per hour and is usually from the southwest. When playing, keep track of the wind speed and direction constantly because it can change at times. If you play the wind properly, you can use it in your favor.

I prefer to play with the wind at my back because I think it helps me play the third shot drop more reliably. In addition, all shots require less effort. However, if I must play into the wind, I will use shots that benefit from this condition, like backspin return of serve shots (because they don't float out of bounds) and body shot attack shots (which are more likely to stay in bounds).

It can be a real headache when the sun is in your face and your opponent is lobbing the ball. In these circumstances, you may have to ask your partner for help or let the ball bounce before hitting it.

If you get stuck facing the sun and wind, request that the teams switch sides midway through the game. For important games, I try to start on the side that I like. I want to do everything possible to get favorable outcomes as quickly as possible.

Power and Control Work Inversely

No matter whether you are trying to hit a queue ball, golf ball, tennis ball, or pickleball, the harder you hit the ball, the less control you have. Weird things happen when you go for 100 percent power. Most coaches say to never exceed 80 percent of your power capability. For almost all shots in pickleball, placement and distance control are more important than power. So, for most shots, you should only hit the ball as hard as is necessary to get the ball to the placement target. When a put-away opportunity arises, don't botch the rally by overpowering and faulting. Instead, use less power, hit your target, and stay in the rally.

CHAPTER 24: SPECIAL SITUATION SHOTS

In this chapter, I'm going to talk about a hodgepodge of valuable though infrequently used shots.

The Fake Overhead Smash (The Overhead Dink)

The fake overhead smash looks just like a put-away smash until the last possible moment when the paddle is almost stopped so that the ball is just lightly tapped. See Figure 24-1. Since the ball falls almost straight down, once it bounces, it almost stays in place. This shot works great in the social arena and against folks with poor mobility. Here is the ideal situation for using this shot.

Your opponents have made a bad lob setting you up for a smash at the NVZ line. Your opponents try to get back. You smash it but they return the smash with another lob that is short, giving you another smash opportunity from the NVZ line. Your

Figure 24-1 The fake overhead smash

opponents are now at or behind the baseline. Now is your chance to use the fake smash. You mimic the exact form you would use for the overhead smash and then dink the ball over the net with the paddle still high.

As with all infrequently used special situation shots, you need to learn how to execute the shot and you need to practice it. You can practice this shot with a wall. Place a piece of painters tape on the wall to mark the top of the net. Hit the ball upward against the wall, sending the ball high and providing your setup. Mimic a smash and then try to dink the ball so that it falls and hits the wall above the net. Do not angle the paddle face downward when contacting the ball. Instead, your tap will likely need a small amount of lift.

The Overhead Misdirection Shot

The misdirection overhead smash looks just like a normal straightforward smash until just before contact when the wrist is then rotated fully counterclockwise (for a right-handed player), thereby angling the paddle face to the right. Most folks expect a smash to go straight forward or slightly left. In this case, the ball kicks to the right. With a little bit of practice with a partner, you should be able to master this shot. So, practice the shot and start using it when your success rate gets to 80 percent or higher.

Other Misdirection Shots

I love the net play elements of disguise, misdirection, head fakes, and juke moves. Such crafty tricks, when practiced and perfected, fake your opponent and help produce winners. I'm lucky to live in a city with many 4.5- and 5.0-rated players who have such tricks. To some extent you can practice these moves using a practice wall. Below are some illustrations that show examples. In Figure 24-2, the paddle is "laid back" at the last moment. Try not to give away your intent by peeking at your target. Figure 24-3 shows a backhand version of the shot where the wrist is laid back in an opposite fashion.

Here's a great way to use the shot shown in Figure 24-2 (misdirection to the right). This is the scenario. You are in the ad court and your opponent has given you an easy forehand dink in front of your right foot. Your far opponent needs to slide toward the middle. Look down the middle and pretend to hit down the middle but lay the paddle back to squirt the ball to the ad court sideline. Unless your far opponent is fast, he can't protect both the middle and the sideline.

Here's a great way to use the shot shown in Figure 24-3 (misdirection to the left). This is the scenario. You are engaged in a backhand crosscourt dinking exchange going from ad court to ad court when your opponent sends a shot to your backhand that is net-high and can be volleyed. Use this backhand misdirection shot to send your shot directly into the upper torso of your near opponent.

The Backhand Stinger

This shot is used for making a sudden backhand shot to the body of the opponent directly across from you.

All visual cues indicate that the shot will go to the left.

Surprise! In a fraction of a second, the paddle changes and the ball goes to the right.

Figure 24-2 Misdirection to the right

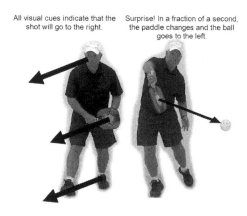

All visual cues indicate that the shot will go to the right.

Surprise! In a fraction of a second, the paddle changes and the ball goes to the left.

Figure 24-3 Misdirection to the left

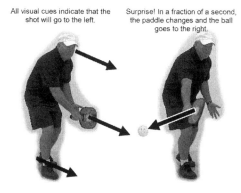

All visual cues indicate that the shot will go to the left.

Surprise! In a fraction of a second, the paddle changes and the ball goes to the right.

Figure 24-4 C-shaped swing to right

Most body shot attacks come from a forehand "slap shot" or "roll shot." Most folks do not expect an attack from the backhand. Here's how to do it. You need to be fully forward at the NVZ line. As always for dinking, you should be compressed and leaning in, ready to volley back any low dink headed for your feet. If your opponent across from you sends over a shot that's a little high, attack it by sliding your open-faced paddle straight forward. Notice the paddle face is open (pointing upward). The quick near-linear stroke action comes from straightening the elbow. You

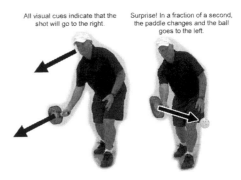

All visual cues indicate that the shot will go to the right.

Surprise! In a fraction of a second, the paddle changes and the ball goes to the left.

Figure 24-5 C-shaped swing to left

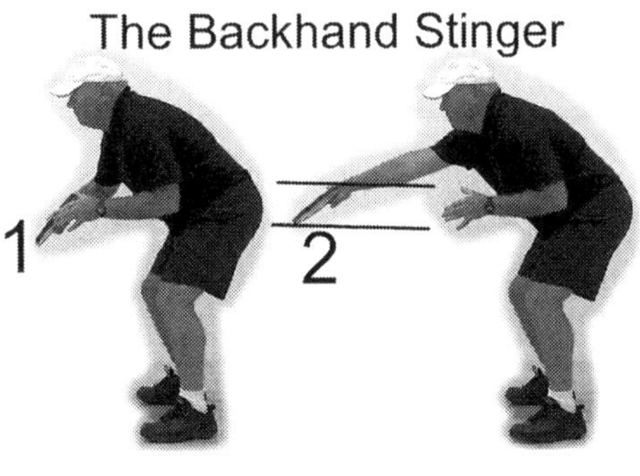

The Backhand Stinger

Figure 24-6 The backhand stinger

can attack successfully with a ball that is a little below net height. You can use a practice wall to perfect the shot. Mark the NVZ line on the floor seven feet back from the wall. Mark the top of the net on the wall. Get compressed, lean in, and feed yourself shots that get slightly higher. When you can volley a ball that is, say, 20 inches high, attack it and try to get your shot to hit the wall about 5 inches above the net. If, in regular game play, you find that this shot gets dodged and goes out of bounds, reduce your power.

The Slap Shot (a.k.a., Body Shot or "Rolling the Ball" at Your Opponent)

A player loses a point when the ball hits him or anything he is wearing. The moment a ball hits your body or clothing, the play is deemed over and the point is awarded to your opponent.

The goal with this shot is to hit your opponent or defeat his reaction time such that he cannot make a good return. Many social players consider such attacks as unsportsmanlike. However, intentionally trying to hit your opponent is considered to be fully acceptable play among advanced competitive players. In fact, the attacked and defeated player typically congratulates the attacker on his or her good shot.

Attack shots are not as easy as you might think, especially when dink shots are kept unattackable. In fact, for players below the 4.5 skill level, most attack shots made against good opponents from a dink bounce fail. Here's why they fail so often. If the shot is fast enough to defeat reaction time, it will likely go out of bounds if dodged. If the shot is slow enough to stay in bounds if dodged, then it is usually slow enough to be attacked. Usually, to be successful with such attack shots made from a dink bounce, you need the following elements.

1. **Good setup.** A good setup is when the ball comes straight to your forehand and makes a high bounce or a bounce near the NVZ line. It's a mistake to attack a ball that is simply unattackable. So, if the ball is low and close to the net, wait for a better setup. The right setup allows brushing upwards on the ball to impart topspin, which helps keep the shot in bounds.

2. **Near-perfect flight line.** There's only a very small window just above the net that allows success. If your shot is outside of the window vertically or horizontally, your opponent can dodge the shot without much effort. Most folks aim too low. The correct start of the trajectory path is essentially right at your opponent's face. However, gravity and topspin will bring the ball down to upper chest height. The ideal spot on your opponent to hit is the right side of the collarbone (right clavicle). For a right-handed player, a shot to the right clavicle is nearly impossible to return.

3. **Disguise and an unready opponent.** Really good players detect attack attempts early and are ready to either play the shot or dodge it. If you make no attempt to disguise your shot, you will likely lose the rally to a savvy opponent. However, if your oppo-

nent is unschooled in attack shots and judging out balls, you can likely win many points with attack shots. Also, if your opponent is holding his or her paddle low, you have a better chance of success.

A common mistake made by the attacker is dumping the shot into the net. Here's what happens. During the acceleration burst forward, the paddle head lags, drops downward, and dumps the shot into the net. You will have to either firm up your wrist to reduce the lag or aim higher to compensate for it.

On the flip side, if you are getting attacked, you need to constantly watch your opponent's paddle, keep your own paddle high, and be compressed and ready to get out of the way of the attack. Keep your dinks unattackable and mainly to opponent backhands. If you see an overzealous player try to get aggressive with an unattackable ball, just dodge it.

In deciding whether to use such attack strategies, you need to think about your other options. If you are good at dinking, it might be smarter to stick with dinking rather than trying an attack or a lob. If your opponents are better than you at dinking, you may have to think about lobs or attacks. As with lobbing, most players underestimate their failures when trying to use the slap shot or any attack strategy from a dink bounce.

CHAPTER 25: ASSESSMENT AND METRICS

A lot of elements are needed for you to be a good pickleball player. You need to have good stroke techniques, you need to know and execute good strategy, and you need to have physical capability.

As said earlier in this book, no matter what the sport is, the path to greatness involves 1) getting expert instruction, 2) practice, practice, and more practice, 3) evaluating results, 4) having the coach define the gaps and needs, and 5) repeating the cycle.

At least several times per year, schedule two hours of private lessons with a good coach. Have the coach look at all parts of your game. Take good notes and make an action plan. All top players in tennis and golf have coaches.

We've already talked about wall practice, partner practice drills, and the need for periodic coaching. What are some other things you can do without the help of others to improve your game?

One thing you can do is try to keep metrics and data.

Assessments: Step 1, Starting Out

Start out by keeping track of serving failures and return of serve failures. Keep a tally through your whole playing period. Initially set a goal of having no more than four or five such failures per two-hour outing. Remember, neither shot needs to be aggressive. Both can be lobs or semi-lobs without harming your game.

Assessments: Step 2, Playing and Defending the Third Shot

Again, in this phase, two things will be measured.

First, after returning the serve, keep track of how many times you failed to be fully forward by the time the third shot came across the net. Hopefully you will be so far forward that you will volley back some shots that would otherwise bounce in the kitchen near the NVZ line. After returning a serve, you should not be fielding the next shot from no man's land. You will be amazed at how many extra points you can earn by being fully forward on time, every time.

Second, rather than counting your third-shot failures, count your third-shot successes. A success is an instance where your third shot bounced before being hit, along with you getting fully forward as a result. So, two things must happen for success: 1) your shot must bounce before being hit, and 2) you have to quickly follow your shot to get fully forward. Short return of serve shots should give you some easy opportunities to drop some third shots in front of your opponent and also allow you to get fully forward.

Assessments: Step 3, Unforced Errors while the Opponent Serving Team is Struggling to Get Fully Forward

Let's say you now have your serve and return of serve working with almost no faults. You are also getting fully forward so fast after returning the serve that you are volleying back shots that would bounce near the NVZ line. You are also making third shots that bounce and you are getting fully forward after many of your third shots.

Now let's start counting and eliminating fourth shot faults and any other faults you incur during the period while your serving team opponents are trying to get forward. Here are some examples of errors.

Your opponents hit a third shot that was high enough to volley back. Your unforced error was either 1) you dumped your shot into the net, 2) you volleyed the shot with too much force, making it go out of bounds, or 3) you volleyed it too high to an opponent's forehand and faulted on his or her fastball return.

In the situation described where you have received a volley shot and your opponents are in a terrible court position, the last thing you should do is botch your shot. Your shot needs to go to the left heel target with a priority of being kept in play.

Assessments: Step 4, Net Play

After all players are fully forward, dinking normally begins. Dinking normally ends due to an error. Either the ball goes into the net or gets popped up and smashed. The errors to be counted are the unforced errors: the shots that went into the net and the shots that got too high. Again, many of these errors result from trying to do too much (like kissing the tape or going for sharp crosscourt angles) instead of just issuing unattackable dinks.

Assessments: Step 5, Advanced Play

To assess advanced play accurately, you need to video record the game or match and then review each rally, perhaps in slow motion. Why? In advanced play, the rallies last longer and the games are longer. It becomes impossible to keep track of what happened and why. In addition, subtle things may be happening that make assessing the root cause of rally failure hard to identify during game play.

In advanced play, the key metrics are about control of the net and control of the ball while dinking. The term control of the net means getting your team fully forward quickly and reliably while also being effective in keeping the opponent team away from the net. Let's get specific. At the top pro level, poor third shots lead directly to a loss of the rally in about 17 percent of instances. In other words, in 17 percent of instances, the serving team could never get fully forward as the result of a poor third shot. The shot could be poor because 1) the third shot goes into the net,

2) the third shot is high and is smashed for a winner, or 3) the third shot is a little high and is attacked, ultimately causing the serving team to fault before getting forward.

So, if you are video recording your games, go through the video and determine the percent of rallies in which your serving team was unable to get fully forward.

Another key metric is how quickly you can get forward following a successful drop shot. At the top pro level, following a successful drop shot into the kitchen, the players can get fully forward before fielding the fourth shot in 54 percent of instances. When they fail to get fully forward after their first drop shot, they can usually get fully forward after their next shot. So, after a good drop shot, a pro will be fully forward 54 percent of the time after the drop shot only, and fully forward 88 percent of the time after either the first drop shot or the first drop shot plus one additional shot.

So, if you are video recording your games, go through the video and determine the percent of instances where you got fully forward after making a drop shot.

In advanced play, assuming all team members are about equal in skill, two things will almost certainly determine the winning team: 1) the team that has the best performance in getting forward quickly and reliably and 2) the team that faults less often at the net (hits fewer pop-ups and shots into the net).

A Simple System
In every game I play, I try to keep track of my unforced errors, such as my shots that go into the net or out of bounds. Even though I am only half of my two-person team, I still find that my unforced error number usually predicts the game outcome.

Summing Up
The best pickleball players know exactly where they stand and what they need to work on. They often video record their matches and later go

through the video rally by rally to understand the failures. They self-assess and they seek expert assessment. They create practice and training programs to address their issues. Mid-level players usually do none of the above.

CHAPTER 26: PREPARING FOR THE BIG TOURNAMENT

Go for it!

Along with practicing and getting coaching, competing is one of the best things you can do to improve your game. Once you register, it will drive you to "get your ducks in a row." You will begin to associate with other competitors, you will learn their tricks, you will start to practice, you will likely seek coaching, and you will learn how to play under stress. I think you will enjoy being part of the group in your town that seeks attaining a high skill level.

I have personally watched about 20 players in my area go from just starting pickleball to becoming 4.5- and 5.0-rated players. They all became much better players through competing.

Here's what you need to do as you prepare for the competition.

Make a list of everything you will need.

Start making this list a few days ahead of the event. Winners don't win by accident. Along with having skill they are organized and responsible. You don't need the stress that comes from trying to throw things together at the last minute. You don't need distractions. One thing that needs to be on the list is the event information—all of the "who, what, when, where," etc. If there is a flyer, make sure it's in the front seat of your car when you depart, along with directions to the event. Put everything on the list you will need, including clothes, hat, water, food, equipment, etc. Bring an extra paddle and extra balls.

Make sure you've done all of your intelligence gathering homework.

To the extent that you can, find out who you will be competing against and start trying to find out who the weakest player is, then seek to learn the weakest player's weakest shot. It may be unavoidable, but you don't want to lose a half dozen points before finally discovering a key weakness.

Plan it all out.

Create a schedule with wake-up time, breakfast, departure, arrival, practice, etc. Make sure the schedule has extra time, prevents rushing, and allows for a relaxing breakfast.

Pack it up beforehand.

Don't start the day of the event off by scurrying and trying to find everything. Pack it all up ahead of time.

Leave early and arrive early.

Leave for the tournament with so much time to spare that not even a terrible wrong turn, faulty GPS, traffic accident, or stop for gas could make you late. There are usually many more competitors than there are courts, making it difficult for latecomers to practice. So, get there early. Practice every shot, especially the third shot drop and lobs. Take into consideration lighting, the backdrop, sun, and wind. Wrap up your practice with enough time to begin intelligence gathering part 2.

Execute intelligence gathering part 2.

As soon as you are able to do so, find out who you will be playing in the first round. If you don't know these folks, try to find somebody who does. Get the skinny if you can and try to watch them practice. Is either player trying to avoid backhands? Is either player left-handed? Do both players appear to be highly mobile? Who's got fast hands and who doesn't? The sooner you can discover the weakest player and his or her weakest shot, the better. If you can learn some things in advance, you might save several points.

Run the early shots on automatic.

Fretting about what they are going to do, other players may freeze up. However, for you, your first several shots are on automatic. You already know where you are going to aim your serve, your return of serve, and your third shot. If you have forgotten, refer back to Chapter 17, which summarizes the first four shots. You also know where and how to dink. Repeat the formula in your mind for the first four shots.

Use the coin toss result wisely.

Often the match begins with a coin toss and the winner gets the choice of first serve or starting side. Sometimes an opponent winning the coin toss is indifferent. If so, express your wishes. If the event is outdoors, there is almost always a superior side due to wind and sun. Even indoors, there is often a superior side based on lighting and backdrop. Just as in outdoor play, I want the strong lighting at my back. If the two sides are exactly equal, pick serving first, as this could provide you with the best chance for an early lead. However, if there is a clearly superior side, choose the side over serving first. I don't want to fight against the sun and wind, even if it may mean that my opponent scores first.

Develop and go through your rituals.

Not knowing what you will do causes anxiety. So, to the extent possible, know what you are going to do. Don't rush a serve. Go through all of your serving rituals. If your partner is serving, go through your ritual of setting yourself up two feet behind the baseline and getting compressed and ready to move. If your partner is receiving the serve, go through your ritual of getting both toes pinned to the NVZ line.

Test your opponents.

As quickly as you can, you need to figure out which opponent has the worst third shot success and if either opponent is slow getting forward after returning the serve. First test the left opponent's backhand. If the first opponent makes a great third shot drop from his or her backhand, return the next serve to the other opponent. Hopefully you will find an opponent who either dumps his or her third shots into the net or sends them long so that they can be volleyed back. If the second opponent also makes a great third shot drop, try going to his or her backhand. One or the other might lose their third shot capability if you apply backspin to your return of serve. Don't "balance things out," but send all return of serves to the opponent with the worse third shot capability. You must be absolutely relentless in exploiting a third shot weakness. If you find an opponent who is slow getting forward after his or her return of serve (which is a godsend in a pickleball tournament), exploit the open net position and put all third shot drops in front of him whenever he is returning the serve. Remember, don't target the kitchen if your opponent is slow and not forward. Instead, clear the net easily and go as deep as possible without giving the opponent a volley shot. So, again, don't try to drop your third shot into the kitchen if there is an open net position. Again, don't be kind and balance things out, but use all opportunities to send third shots to the slow opponent who is providing the open net position.

Play your game, not theirs.

Hopefully you know your strengths and weaknesses and what style of play best suits your skill set. Try to play the game you are best at. If it gets off base, steer it back. Here's an example. I can usually win a rally if it becomes a matter of who can dink the longest without faulting. The slow game is my strength. My weakness is volley wars. The last thing I want to do is open up a fastball fight. If a volley fight breaks out, I often look for an opportunity to return their volley with a dink by taking pace off of the ball.

Focus on the here, the now, and the ball.
This is why you need to get all of the logistical things taken care of well in advance. You've got to be constantly "in the moment." Narrow your thinking to include just you and the ball.

If it ain't broke, don't fix it. Don't change a winning game.
Some folks would say that it's okay to try new things once you have a nice lead. For some sports, after a certain point, it can become impossible for a loser to win before the clock runs out. But pickleball has no clock. Don't start trying new things because you have a lead. The games are too short, the points are too precious, and many points are often scored quickly in streaks.

Never give an inch.
Never let up or give your opponent any type of break, even if you are winning by 10 to 0. Pickleball can be streaky and fortunes can change quickly. If there is a weak opponent, exploit the situation without mercy. If an opponent can't retrieve lobs, lob without mercy.

Break their momentum by calling a timeout.
Don't be afraid to stop the game when things aren't going your way. Opponent success builds confidence, which can build more success. On the flip side, frustration can build and it hurts more as it builds. In some sports, it has been statistically validated that timeouts indeed work and alter momentum. Talk with your partner, take a rest, and discuss any needed adjustments.

Make adjustments if necessary.
Let's suppose you are playing the game you are good at and you are playing your game great, but it is apparent that you will be beaten by playing this game. In other words, you are simply getting beat at your own preferred way of playing. We've all seen mid-game adjustments that turn things around. Often times the second half of a football game looks noth-

194

ing like the first half. For me, lobbing can often help turn things around. I think my soft game is my best, but if I'm getting beaten using it, I sometimes switch and find that my fastball fighting is better than my opponent's fastball fighting. Also, remember the key countermeasures.

What's Happening	Countermeasure
You are getting attacked with body shots.	Watch his paddle and whether he's trying to attack unattackable balls. Dodge the attacks being made from unattackable dink bounces. Keep your dinks to the backhand. Avoid the attacker if there is only one.
You are having trouble handling fastballs from bangers.	Don't hit out balls. Don't try to block a fastball that is higher than your upper torso because it will likely go out of bounds. If your opponent is banging from the baseline, drop the ball into the kitchen using a block dink. Block other shots to the left heel target. Keep shots to your opponent's backhand.
They are getting lobs past you.	Watch your opponent's paddle closely and move back before the lob ever occurs. As soon as he takes his eyes off of you, take two quick steps back to prepare for the overhead. To prevent lobs, avoid the lobber, or hit to the side he is not lobbing from. Keep your opponents moving and reaching.

CHAPTER 27: THE COLLECTED WISDOM OF COACH MO AND FINAL BOOK SUMMARY

The two authors of this book (Joe and Mo) organize and present material in completely opposite ways. Coach Mo writes in lists of "one liners." His wisdom comes in numbered lists and short bullet points. This summary is mainly in the Coach Mo style. You may recognize the lists and points. Much of this material comes from the Pickleball Coach web site (http://pickleballcoach.com), created by Coach Mo.

Part 1 – Fundamentals & Techniques

The Grip

1. Use the Continental grip for all shots. When the grip is correct, the point of the V between your thumb and index finger should be placed on top of the handle of the paddle when the face of the paddle is perpendicular to the ground.
2. The Continental grip is halfway between the Eastern Forehand Grip and the Eastern Backhand Grip used by tennis players. A player should not change his or her grip during a rally. No matter whether forehand or backhand, the volley, the serve, overheads, and ground strokes should all use the Continental grip.

3. Most pickleball players only keep one hand on the paddle when making their shots. A player can have much greater control hitting the ball if he uses two hands to steady the paddle before hitting the ball. Pro tennis players almost always have two hands on the racquet between hits.

4. If you have a wet grip problem on hot, humid days, wear a wrist band and buy some tennis over grips for your paddle handle. Over grips are inexpensive and easy to install.

Ready Position

1. Get back to the ready position quickly after every stroke. For volleys, keep your paddle up and in front of your body and "reload" quickly after a hit.

2. A common mistake made while moving forward to the net is not having your paddle in proper ready position. Many players have their paddles at their knees or below the net, not up and out in front of the body.

3. At the point when the ball contacts your opponent's paddle, you should be stopped and in the split step ready position. Check points: elbows and paddle out in front of your body, feet at least shoulder width apart, on your toes not your heels, ready to move left or right. Never be moving when your opponent contacts the ball. No matter where you are on the court, stop and get into your ready position. Never sacrifice being ready for a better position on the court. No matter where you are on the court, if you are not prepared early and properly to hit the ball, you probably will not hit a good shot.

The Serve

1. Don't miss your serve more than once per month.

2. When serving the ball, give yourself leeway. Aim for the center of the serving box five feet from the baseline. Serve fast only if you never miss your serve.

3. Never miss your serve because you are hitting too hard. Practice! Your opponents only need a pulse to win the point if you miss the serve. Give them a chance to lose. Also, your partner will lose confidence in you if you keep missing your serve.

4. Spot your target and get aligned. Your target should be the very center of the serving box. This will give you a wide margin for error. Bend your knees. Point your paddle toward the ground. Drop the ball from above. Use a bowling motion. Step toward the target with your front shoulder pointing at your target. Swing in an upward motion with the paddle below the wrist and watch the ball contact your paddle below the waist. Make a soft sound to yourself at the point of contact with the ball to prevent you from lifting your head before contact. Follow through in the direction of your target.

5. After serving, get back one step behind the baseline. The return of serve could come back deep and it's difficult to hit a good third shot if you are moving backwards. Also, if you are standing in the court, you cannot determine if the return of serve shot might land out of bounds.

6. If your opponent has the ability to hit a drop shot as his or her return of serve, be prepared to quickly run forward.

The Return of Serve

1. Wait for the serve a step or more behind the baseline so that the ball will bounce in front of you, not at your feet, causing a difficult shot. If your opponent has a very fast and deep serve, you may have to wait about three feet behind the baseline.

2. Never try for a pure winner on a return of serve. Do not make an unforced error.

3. When your opponents have equal skill, make your target spot five feet from the baseline and eight inches left of center. This will keep the ball closer to the backhand of the left opponent, whose backhand is toward the middle of the court (for a right-handed

player). For this target, the ball will travel over the low part of the net. Give yourself a margin for error and hit the ball slowly to give you plenty of time to set up at the NVZ line.

4. If one opponent is weaker than the other with third shot capability, hit the return to the weak opponent's backhand.

5. If you have the capability, change spin occasionally (top or under spin). It will cause some opponents to make mistakes at times.

6. When a good opportunity presents, surprise your opponent and hit a drive return of serve. Place this shot down the middle, slightly closer to the backhand player. Both opponents may think the other will take the shot.

7. Watch for a short serve or a serve to the outer corner. Keep a mental note of players who hit such serves. Watch the face of the server's paddle and be ready to sprint in and split your feet for the short return.

The Third Shot

When your serve is returned, try to place a soft shot that will bounce in front of your opponent. A low soft shot is important because it gives you time to get to the net and not be on the defensive. Spend time practicing this shot. It is the most important shot in the game.

Ground Stroke Stances

Ground strokes can be hit from an open or a closed stance, depending on how much time you have to set up. When starting behind the baseline, as when waiting for the serve or return of serve, you should have enough time to use the classic, closed stance with the feet and body turned sideways to the net. This stance ensures complete and proper shoulder and body turn. The player runs to a spot where the ball will be as close to waist high as possible and sets his feet shoulder width apart, sideways to the net. He then steps toward the ball with his front foot and hits the ball.

After making the third shot, almost anytime you are playing in no man's land, there will not be enough time to set up in a closed position.

So, the open stance is used when you have very little time to move your feet. Still, you need to turn your upper body at the waist so that your front shoulder is pointing at your target area. A right-handed player hitting a forehand would point his or her left shoulder toward the target, and when hitting a backhand would point his or her right shoulder toward the target. The follow-through is also toward the target.

The Forehand Ground Stroke

1. Move to the ball early.
2. With your left hand, help guide the paddle back into position, aimed and ready to push straight forward through the strike.
3. Step toward the ball with your left foot and make contact with the ball opposite the lead toe. Point your left shoulder at your target.
4. For balance, keep your left hand in front of your body with your palm facing the ground at the same height as your paddle.
5. Watch the ball make contact with your paddle and make a sound to yourself at the exact moment the ball touches your paddle. This will help you watch the ball more consistently.
6. Keep a firm wrist and pretend you are hitting four balls lined up in a row during your follow through. Follow through in the direction of your target.
7. When hitting a low forehand shot, bend your knees with your right knee as close to the ground as possible, then stay down all the way through the shot.
8. Quickly return to your ready position.

The Backhand Groundstroke

1. Move to the ball early. Run to a spot where the ball will be waist high or as close to waist high as possible and get in your ready position.
2. Set your feet in a closed stance position (side by side) pointing your right shoulder and looking over your right shoulder toward your target, then step with your front foot toward your target.

3. If the ball is low, bend your knees to meet the ball low and allow you to keep your paddle tip up. Keep your head and body down all through the shot and follow through.
4. The contact point should be in front of your body, even with the lead toe.
5. Keep a firm wrist through the strike.
6. Watch the ball hit your paddle. Make a sound to yourself at the moment you see contact.
7. Make a long follow through in the direction of your target. Pretend you are hitting four balls in a row.
8. After your full follow through, quickly get back to your ready position for the next shot.

Footwork Notes

1. Avoid stepping into the NVZ with both feet. If the ball should bounce close to the net, keep one foot planted behind the NVZ line and lunge forward with the other like a sword fighter. Dink the ball over the net into your opponents' kitchen area and quickly recover and get both feet behind your NVZ line. If a player steps into the kitchen with both feet, it will take twice as long to get back out. A player who has stepped into the kitchen is vulnerable to an attack, and will fault if he can't get both feet established behind the NVZ line before the attack occurs.
2. At the NVZ line, side shuffle steps are ideal to protect your ready position base. However, for less mobile players, a side step first combined with a cross step is sometimes necessary and effective. Step toward the post in either direction and cross step when the ball is hit out of your reach. Do not move your back foot and lose your position on the court. Cross stepping makes you a foot taller and gives you a wider range of coverage. When making a cross step, make sure your dink stays close to the net.
3. No matter where you are on the court, always split step, putting your feet side by side and shoulder width apart, at the moment

your opponent contacts the ball. This allows you to move in either direction equally well. Do not sacrifice being balanced and ready in an attempt to gain a better position on the court.

Volley Techniques & Strategies

1. When you are waiting for the ball, you should be in the ready position. Your elbows should be in front of your body, your feet should be at least shoulder width apart, and you should be on your toes. The head of your paddle should be higher than your wrist. You should see wrinkles on your wrist. Never drop the head of your paddle and let those wrinkles disappear. The angle of the face of the paddle should be slightly open (1 o'clock to 7 o'clock).

2. Bend your knees on all low shots. Your back knee and the butt of the paddle may be almost touching the ground. Stay down all the way through your shot and keep your head down and eyes looking at the contact point long after the ball is gone.

3. Try to keep your head and eyes behind the ball at ball height when hitting a volley.

4. Beginner pickleball players have a tendency to swing at their volleys and punch their ground strokes, but it should be just the opposite. There is not enough time to swing at most volleys and you lose your consistency when you swing and don't punch. You punch the shot by extending your arm from the elbow. Do not swing at your volleys unless you are an advanced player and feel you can make 80 percent of your swinging volleys. Punch them unless your opponent hits a very fast volley or overhead at close range at you. Then just set the height and angle of your paddle and block the shot low to your opponent's feet.

5. When you punch your ground strokes, you lose power and control. Stroke your ground strokes for better placement and power.

6. When you strike the ball, you should point your front shoulder in the direction you want the ball to go and open or close the face of the paddle to set the angle of the paddle. Keep a firm wrist and

extend your arm from only the elbow joint, using a jab motion. Setting the angle of the paddle and the jab motion are two completely separate motions. First aim the paddle early. Then jab from the elbow joint.

7. Keep the butt of the paddle traveling parallel to the ground all the way through the jab to create a linear paddle path. Adjust and aim the paddle face before the strike.

8. Don't get crowded by the ball. Always make contact with the ball as far out in front of your body as you can to get more power and control of placement and placement angles.

9. At the exact point of contact with the ball make a sound to yourself. This will help prevent you from making one of the biggest mistakes made while playing pickleball: not watching the ball all the way to the paddle.

10. After the point of contact, keep your eyes focused on the contact point during your follow through.

11. Return to the ready position quickly after each volley. The harder you hit your volley, the faster you must return to the ready position.

12. If you don't have time to step to the ball, at least turn your upper body and point your front shoulder in the direction you want the ball to go. If you don't have time to turn your shoulders, then from the ready position keep a stationary wrist with the paddle parallel to the net and block the shot over the net.

13. Whenever the ball is high enough to direct it downward, do so as a first priority. If you can, direct your volley low to your opponent's feet or bounce the ball on the court exactly beside him.

14. If you can't hit downward, a good target is your right-handed opponent's right clavicle, as this forces an awkward paddle position.

15. If you are not fully forward, after each volley shot, move forward one step toward the NVZ until you are fully forward.

16. On the backhand volley keep your knuckles lined up with the paddle face in the direction you want the ball to go and keep the

handle slightly ahead of the paddle.

17. You must use an aggressive jab when volleying a ball with a heavy spin.

18. The difference between an overhead and a volley is based on the height at which you can contact the ball. If the ball is below the highest point at which you can reach it with the center of your paddle, you should use a volley shot. If it is above that point, you should hit an overhead shot. If you use the overhead technique when the ball is too low, you will not be able to fully extend your arm and you will probably put the ball in the net.

19. When at the net, turn toward your opponent before he hits the ball. When the ball travels straight toward your paddle it is easier to hit than when it comes in at an angle.

The Overhead

1. To hit a good overhead shot, you need to set up behind the ball with your body sideways to the target. But, do not run backwards (back pedaling). Instead, for safety, turn sideways and side step back to the ball. When setting up, if you don't have time to move your feet, at least turn your shoulders and waist to achieve more power and placement consistency.

2. On a high, deep lob, sidestep back past your anticipated contact point and then step forward into the shot. Having forward momentum into the shot will give you more power and consistency.

3. Never hit an overhead shot unless the ball is high enough. You should hit the ball at the highest point you can reach (full extension) with the ball at the center of your paddle. If the ball is too low to allow a full arm extension, you should make a volley shot instead. A rather high floating ball could allow you to make an aggressive swinging volley shot downward.

4. The difference between an overhead and a volley is based on the height at which you can contact the ball. If the ball is below the

highest point at which you can reach it with the center of your paddle, you should use a volley shot. If it is above that point, you should hit an overhead shot. If you use the overhead technique when the ball is too low, you will not be able to fully extend your arm and you will probably put the ball in the net.

5. When hitting an overhead shot, point your shoulder and a finger of your left hand at the ball until just before you contact the ball. Keep your head up until the ball is long gone. Pronate your wrist and paddle just before you contact the ball to create a more disguised and powerful overhead. Aim at the near opponent's feet.

6. When the wind is at your back, your timing can be thrown off by the ball drifting forward. This can cause the ball to go into the net. To help with this problem, aim your overheads inside the baseline with a margin for error.

7. Keep in mind while hitting the overhead: 1) use your palm to block the sun, 2) keep your paddle face flat for power, and 3) point your finger at the ball. If your finger moves forward, step forward and vice-versa.

8. Run back parallel to the flight of the ball if it is hit straight over your head.

9. To get maximum power, make sure that the paddle face is completely flat at the point of contact.

10. Keep your head and chin up and watch the spot where the ball contacts the paddle long after your follow through.

11. The overhead technique requires a snap of the wrist. Just step towards your target, point your left shoulder towards the target, and snap your wrist with the same motion as you would snap a whip. Pretend you are throwing the paddle at the ball.

Offensive and Defensive Lobs

1. When making a lob, lob over your opponent's backhand side. This way, if the lob is short, you will get a backhand response rather than a hard forehand smash.

2. If you hit a very high, short lob (a poor lob) from close to the net and you are exceptionally fast on your feet, then the high percentage action is to get behind the baseline and play your opponent's overhead. If you are not able to quickly retreat to the baseline, then hold your position at the net with your paddle in the ready (blocking) position. If the ball is hit at your feet while you are stuck in no man's land, it is almost impossible to return. Do not leave your position at the net unless you are 100 percent confident that you can retreat to the baseline with enough time to prepare for your opponent's overhead.

3. If the ball is lobbed over your head at the net, your partner should yell, "I've got it," and run behind you. At the same time, you should switch sides of the court. However, if you feel you can make a good overhead, call off your partner quickly, saying, "I've got it."

4. If a ball is hit straight over your head and your partner isn't running back to help you, then run back parallel to the ball so when you get to the ball, you can hit a deep forehand lob. Do not turn 180 degrees and run straight back after the ball, because you will not be in a good position to hit the ball when you get to it.

5. Hit a few high lobs before every game to evaluate the direction of the wind and its speed. During every second of an important game, keep the wind direction in mind. It will give you points. Steady your game by playing the wind to your advantage. Beginner and intermediate players would hit less out balls if they hit into the wind. Advanced players are better qualified to play the wind. It can help you and hurt you.

6. If the wind is 20 mph or greater, it is best to have it at your back.

The Drop Volley (The Drop Shot)

1. A good time to play the drop volley shot is when your opponent is moving away from the net near the baseline or if your opponent never comes to the net. A perfect time to use this shot is after your opponent has chased a lob and then remains near the baseline.

2. Most drop volleys are placed near the post on the side of the court from which your opponent has just retreated to field a lob. In such a case, if you think his or her partner has been anticipating your drop volley, don't place your drop volley by the post. Instead, place it halfway between the net and the baseline so that the net person must run away from the net to play the ball. It is much more difficult to hit a shot when moving quickly away from the net than toward the net. Many times the player who just ran way back for the lob will recover and get in the way of his partner trying to help him out.

3. Don't use the drop volley shot until you have practiced it. Many players fault frequently with this shot. Invest the time to learn the shot.

4. The paddle motion is from high to low like the shape of a half moon. The paddle face finishes parallel to the ground. Do not chop downward because this requires extremely precise timing.

5. Slide your paddle under the ball, like turning a key in a door, to put an under spin on the ball. The ball will check up when it drops over the net.

6. At the point of contact on a touch shot, squeeze your pinky, middle finger, and ring finger together. This will help you keep a firm wrist.

7. This is a shot where you must get beneath the ball. So bend your knees and get low.

8. The shot uses a short backswing and then elbow straightening through the stroke.

9. Punch the ball, which requires the full extension of the elbow joint.

10. Meet the ball early and out in front of your body.

11. Do not drop the paddle head below your wrist. If the paddle face is locked firmly above your wrist then you can see skin wrinkles on your wrist.

12. Keep your head down and eyes glued to the spot that you made

contact with the ball for as long as possible.

13. The paddle head should follow through in the direction you want the ball to go.

14. Make a sound to yourself at exactly the time the ball makes contact with your paddle: not too soon or too late. This will make sure you are watching the ball hit the paddle.

How to Practice

If you want to move from being a good player to a great player, you must understand the importance of practice. Find a partner who appreciates the importance of practice.

1. Practice footwork. A player should learn proper footwork to become a better player. Learn to cross step, side step, shuffle sideways, and split step. Good footwork makes for easier court coverage, wider range, better balance, and better shots.

2. Net play requires patience. You must practice a soft game at the net until you can do it for five minutes without faulting.

3. Break the game down into segments and practice each segment. Examples follow.

4. Ground strokes. Practice corner to corner and down the line.

5. Volleys and drop volleys. Practice with one player at the net and the other at the baseline. Volley balls hit from different angles, speeds, and distances.

6. Lobs and overheads. One player lobs the ball to a player at the net, who hits overhead shots from different locations.

7. Play points out using half of the doubles court. Go from corner to corner, not keeping score and without serving and then with serving. Points should not be counted because a player tends to try to win by doing only the things that he does well, rather than practicing things he doesn't do well.

8. After practicing for a long period of time, play a singles match using only half of the doubles court and keeping score (sometimes called skinny singles). Try to move your opponent around

the court and out of position with ball placement and the other strategies presented earlier.

9. After practicing the whole game in segments, the game then becomes an extension of practice and you should play better pickleball.

Part 2 – Strategy Elements

Poaching

To poach is to cut off and hit the shot that your opponent intended to go to your partner. Often, the third shot is poached by the service return team because one player is already fully forward in a good position for poaching. Another good time to poach is during a crosscourt dinking exchange. If the shot intended for opponent A gets a little high, opponent B might cut it off with a poach.

It is important to pick the proper time in the game to poach. Early in the game is ideal so that you can rattle your opponents while still having time to recover in case you lose the point. Another good time is when your team is way ahead (can afford to take a risk) or way behind (must change something in order to win). Below are some key points.

1. Make sure that your opponents are worried that you may poach. You are not doing your job if you are not giving head and shoulder fakes at the net. Occasionally poach just to make your fakes seem believable.

2. Here's a way to make your opponent hit the ball to you. Make a head and shoulder fake in one direction and hold your position on the court. Your opponent will think that you are going to move down the net and he will often hit the ball to you. Occasionally you will have to poach to make your fakes believable.

3. Here is a common situation. Your opponents are both strong but you have a weak partner. If the game is important, if you poach or can fake a poach, you can help level the playing field.

4. An excellent poacher should poach as much as possible. His or her partner should not take this as a personal affront. It is proper play and good strategy.

5. Strategy #1: Wait at the net until you see an easy-to-poach return from your opponent. Then move across the court to cut the shot off for a winner.

6. Strategy #2: You anticipate, perhaps because the ball is headed to a backhand, an easy-to-poach return. You take a risk and move to cut the shot off a split second before your opponent hits the ball.

7. Strategy #3: You see that your opponent is fielding a very difficult shot, such as a shot to the left heel target. So, you predict that the return will be weak and move to cut it off.

8. Strategy #4: You use a preplanned and practiced signal to your partner to let him know you will move to his net position, while he moves to your position.

Hitting Down the Sideline

Trying to drive the ball down the sideline when you are located deep in the court is usually low percentage play. People overestimate their placement capability. Unless the down-the-line hole is huge, don't get suckered into this shot. The Coach Mo advice is as follows.

1. Do not hit shots down the sideline unless:
   - Your opponents poach.
   - Your team is favored to win and your team has a good lead.
   - You have an easy ball to hit (such as one perfectly placed for a forehand roll).
   - You want to keep your opponents honest when they are close to center court. In other words, your opponents are providing a huge hole along the sideline.
   - Your opponent's backhand is to the outside of the court and he is the weaker player.

2. A soft shot down the line is just as good, if not better, than a fastball, especially if you can bounce the ball beside your opponent and be ready to jump on any return that is about a foot higher than the net.

3. If you are stretched out toward a sideline when volleying, always go down the near sideline. The shot will have more power and be

more consistent than a crosscourt attempt. This follows from the baseball advice of "going with the pitch." When the pitch goes to the outside of the plate, go for a hit to right field instead of trying to pull the ball toward the center. Follow through a little shorter for a straight volley down the sideline.

Playing the Wind

Whether you prefer to play with the wind or against it is a personal choice. There is no right or wrong choice. It depends on your abilities with respect to the wind.

1. A light, steady wind in your face is excellent for a person who likes to lob. The wind will blunt the trajectory and hold the ball in bounds.

2. A heavy wind in your face is not good for lobbing because it would likely give your opponent many overhead smash opportunities.

3. A heavy wind at your back is an advantage to a hard hitter because it could add 15–20 mph to their stroke, making it much harder for their opponent to react.

4. If the wind is coming across the court sideways, you must stay away from the side of the court toward which the wind is blowing. Keep the wind on your mind at all times.

5. If winds are gusty, you must monitor the wind frequently and play it properly.

6. Try to convince yourself the wind is bothering your opponent as much as it is bothering you.

7. Play the wind wisely and better than your opponent and this may help you win.

How to Judge "Out Balls"

An "out ball" is a shot that will land out of bounds if you can restrain yourself from hitting it. Judging out balls is a vital skill, and it's a skill that separates 4.0-rated players from 5.0-rated players. Usually a fast shot coming at shoulder height will fly out of bounds. At the net, a fast shot hit from below the net will usually fly out of bounds. When your opponent tries to attack you from an unattackable dink, if you dodge the shot, it will likely go out of bounds. Here are some important considerations.

1. Is the wind at your opponent's back?
2. Is your opponent swinging fast at a ball below the net?
3. Is your opponent making a difficult shot while running?
4. Listen to and obey a "no" call from your partner.
5. When you find an opponent who can't judge out balls and who swings at everything, capitalize on the fault and attack him.
6. Be aware of where you are on the court at all times. This will help you decide whether to hit a shot that might go out of bounds.
7. If you stop hitting your opponents' out balls your percentage of wins will rise immediately.

Intelligence Gathering, Knowing Your Opponents

In tournament or league play where the outcome of the game really matters, you need to do your homework and learn about your opponents in advance. You need to find out from other players the strengths and weaknesses you will face. If you are able to do so, you need to watch your opponents play before you face them in a match. Games are too short to figure out opponents' weaknesses on the fly.

Key things you need to know include:

1. Is he good with the third shot or does he just bang it?
2. Is he reliable in dinking or will he flub it or pop it up after a few hits?
3. Can he cover the court and get lobs and short shots, or does he have mobility issues?
4. Does he have fast hands and good fastball handling capability or do fastballs make him fault?
5. Does he try to hit everything or does he know how to dodge out balls?
6. Does he lob and can he lob reliably?
7. Does he get to the line on time following a service return or does he leave a large window for the third shot?

8. Can he handle return of serves that have heavy backspin or does he dump such shots into the net?
9. Does he poach and, if so, does he move before the ball is hit?

From this information, you can develop a strategy before the game starts. Even at the pro level, one player is always weaker. You and your partner need to agree on who to "pick on" and how to exploit player weaknesses before the match begins.

In the information era we live in now, a savvy player should be able to ferret out information before the day of the match.

Mental Errors

Many mental mistakes come from inexperience. Hopefully most of these will disappear as you gain experience and poise. Mental errors include many, many things like:

1. What shot am I supposed to use and where do I place it?
2. Oh no. I forgot I'm not supposed to reach so high and I hit an out ball.
3. Over hitting. I had a huge hole and I over hit and went out of bounds.
4. Not enough patience. I could have won the dinking battle, but I went for an attack shot that went out of bounds.
5. Not keeping track of the wind.
6. Not having a mental book on your opponents' assets and deficits.
7. Not communicating properly with your partner.
8. Being so predictable that your opponents take advantage of it.

Reducing Unforced Errors

As discussed earlier in this book, in pickleball, you do not have the control and capability that you think you have. As a consequence, the ball seems to end up everywhere except where you want it to go. Even at the highest levels of play, the team with the fewest unforced errors usually wins the game. Being careful, keeping the ball in play, and waiting for the put-away opportunity are hallmarks of smart play. Here are some tips.

1. The safe spot. When all players are forward, the safest shot is to bounce the ball low and in the middle of the NVZ near the net. Such a shot is not very attackable. With this placement, your opponent may hesitate, thinking that his partner will hit the ball. Hit the ball softly so your opponents must add their own pace to the ball.

2. When at the net be patient. Keep hitting the ball softly and into the NVZ until your opponents make the mistake of hitting the ball too high. Be defensive and give your opponent unattackable dink shots. Do not go for the kill unless the ball is at least 12 inches above the net. Eighty-five percent of your shots should be dinks and low volleys made while your toes are pinned to the NVZ line. Do not try to kiss the tape, and avoid trying to make tough crosscourt shots.

3. If the ball gets high, angle your paddle down and try to bounce the ball between your opponents. This is a better choice than trying to angle the shot toward a sideline.

4. Learn how to make offensive lobs. They can be effective against many opponents.

5. If you hit a fast volley to your opponent, you must prepare your paddle face for the next shot faster. The faster you hit, the faster you must prepare.

6. Only try angle shots if you get a high "floater" and feel that you are 150 percent sure that you won't make an unforced error.

7. Don't try to win the game from deep in the court using ground strokes. Ground strokes are usually only used when returning a serve, making a third shot, or fielding a lob that has bounced.

8. Always allow a margin for error. Never aim for the line itself.

9. If you cannot make a specific shot at least eight out of ten times, do not try this shot in a game. Four out of ten tries is just enough to lose the game. Shot selection at key times in the game is very important. Know the shots that you are very consistent with and use them at key times in the game.

10. Give your opponents a chance to lose. Don't beat them to it.

11. When warming up before your pickleball game, hit a couple of high lobs to check out the wind direction and speed. Don't lose points during a game trying to figure these things out. In addition, practice third shots before the match begins.

Extras, Advice, and Miscellaneous Strategies

1. When you are learning to play pickleball, never avoid hitting your backhand ground strokes, dinks, and volleys. If you avoid hitting your backhand you will never master the stroke. You can use wall practice to quickly develop your backhand capability. If you lack backhand strength, you can use an inexpensive resistance band to build strength. Just make your backhand stroke against the resistance of the band. Some folks try to avoid using the backhand by reaching across their body low or high with the forehand. Such shots do not work well.

Trying to avoid playing a backhand shot by reaching across low or reaching across high does not work.

Figure 26-1 Don't avoid your backhand, Trying to avoid playing a backhand by reaching across low or reaching across high does not work.

2. When you are feeling a little tight during a match, don't hit tentatively or too slowly. Hit at your normal steady pace, but give yourself more leeway to hit your target until your confidence returns.

3. Make a mental book on your own attributes and deficits. Only hit shots that you feel are a high percentage for your own ability. Play

the game and make the shots that you do well and practice the things that you don't do well until they become high percentage options.

4. Bounce up onto the balls of your feet, in the ready position, at the point of contact of the ball on your opponent's paddle. A moving body reacts quicker than a stationary body.

5. Split step every time your opponent touches the ball.

6. If your shot makes your opponent take two steps or more, your chance of winning the point increases immensely.

7. Don't back up to play a dink off the bounce when you can hit the ball as a low volley.

8. When playing anywhere away from the net, always try to hit the ball with your weight moving forward and try to gain at least a step or two toward the net. However, if you give your opponent a very attackable high shot by mistake, get behind the baseline if you can.

9. Pick a good time to move forward, not when your opponent can attack your shot. Every second that you are playing, if you are not fully forward, your goal should be to get to the net. When you hit a successful shot into the kitchen, you must advance quickly, getting at least halfway to the net.

10. Make contact with the ball at the highest possible point in the air when volleying, and waist high on the bounce for your ground strokes. Catching the ball high opens up more angles and reduces the chance of hitting into the net.

11. Give your opponents a lot of chances to miss and they will not let you down.

12. Play steady. Patience is a virtue in pickleball. The team with the most unforced errors will almost always lose the game.

13. It is not how hard you hit the ball, but where. Power is beneficial for some shots, but for most shots, placement is more important than power. Only hit the ball as hard as you can control the placement. Do not sacrifice good placement by using too much power. Hit ¾ winners unless you get a put-away shot for a full power winner.

14. The harder you hit the ball, the sooner it will come back. So, whenever you hit the ball hard, you must get ready quickly. Assume that your hard shots will come back across the net.

15. Expect to win and refuse to give up or back off.

16. Keep the ball as low as possible for every hit, unless you must make a defensive lob.

17. Place the ball at your opponent's feet or bounce the ball right beside your opponent. He must hit the ball up, which quickly puts him on the defensive and you on the offensive. The team which must hit the ball up most of the time will lose. Keep the ball at your opponent's feet no matter where he is on the court.

18. When an opponent is planted at the net and you can't make a shot at his feet, the next best place to hit it is at the right hip pocket or right clavicle of a right-handed player.

19. Do not try to win the point from the baseline. Just hit the ball softly and bounce the ball in the NVZ and follow it to the net.

20. If your partner is drawn out of the court on his side, you must move over to protect his area until he can get back into the court. Another option is to give a head and shoulder fake, giving the impression that you are moving to cover for your partner. Don't actually move from your position, however, and your opponent will probably hit the ball to you.

21. If you feel an opponent is anticipating your shot by watching the face of your paddle and moving before you make contact, you may need to add disguise. Hold your paddle face straight ahead and then, at the last second, aim toward your target.

22. If you are playing a former racquetball player (who very quickly flicks his paddle at the ball), you must prepare your ready position even earlier.

23. Be a good model of integrity. No game is worth more than your integrity. If you agree with your partner's line call (in or out), echo your agreement. If your view is good and you see that your partner makes an incorrect line call (i.e., the ball is good, but he called

it out), express your view to your partner. The lack of consensus will go in favor of your opponent. If you can't make a call, ask for help or concede the rally. Going further, a player should call out his own shots if the player clearly sees the ball out regardless of whether requested to do so by an opponent. All players should cooperate to attain accurate line calls.

24. Before starting each game, let your partner know that you don't mind his overruling any call you make as long as he is 100 percent sure you were wrong. If one person on a team feels a ball was in and the other doesn't, then the point goes to the other team. If your feelings about the score or whether the ball is in or out are different from the other three players on the court, then right or wrong, you should concede.

25. Every once in a while, change the spin and speed of all your shots. The element of surprise will pay dividends.

26. Sometimes the best shot is no shot at all. When playing with a much better partner than yourself, let your partner take as many shots as he possibly can, especially if he yells, "I have it." Chances are good you are probably going to get the lion's share of all the hits anyway. So the more your partner touches the ball, the better chance you will win. Also, try to give smash opportunities to the forehand player, even if the forehand player has to move onto your court to field it. Everybody loves to smash the ball, but you need to give the shot to the player who can make a better shot.

27. There should be only positive communication between you and your partner. Examples: "Great shot," "Good job."

28. Remember the vital communications, such as, "I have it," "yours," "switch," "it's good," "no," "stay back," and "bounce it."

29. The second to last shot before the end of a point by you or your partner usually decides if your team either wins or loses the point. If you do not keep your shot low enough or placed well enough and your opponent slams a shot at your partner and he misses the shot, then the point was lost by you. Sometimes the point could

have been lost by the third or fourth to last shot because the team never could recover from being put on the defensive earlier in the point.

30. Keep a book in your mind about the people whom you play regularly. Know what they are good at and also know their weaknesses. Many players always make certain shots in particular situations, and if you can anticipate these shots, you will have an edge. For example, some players, when running in for a ball that bounces near the post in the NVZ, always try a crosscourt topspin shot to the other post.

31. Also keep a book on your own strengths and weaknesses. It helps to really know your fault rates and success rates with shots such as lobs and drop shots.

32. When your team is a heavy favorite, play a whole game without being interested in winning and concentrate on just placing every single ball at your opponent's feet or beside them. Practice not going for winners and being patient. No matter where your opponents are on the court, go for their feet. It is a safe shot, and it will steady your game and pay dividends.

33. On a crosscourt volley make contact a little farther out in front of you.

34. All strokes taken with your pickleball paddle are technically the same as all the tennis strokes with one exception: the serve. The only differences between the two are the feel of the ball on the paddle and the distance from your hand to the contact point of the ball on the paddle. A person wanting to improve his pickleball strokes should read tennis books and magazines and become a student of the game.

35. Learn all the proper tennis stroking techniques to help improve your pickleball game.

36. If two players with the same natural ability play pickleball and one uses the proper tennis technique, that player will be a steadier and better player.

37. Determine if your opponents are left-handed before the start of the game so that you won't be hitting to their strength.

38. Never yell anything that may help your opponent. For example, say that you have just overpowered a shot and see that it is going out of bounds. Don't yell in disgust because your opponent may hit your out ball if you do not bring it to his attention that you are frustrated with your shot.

39. If both players are self-taught players then the one with the most athletic sense and ability will be the better player. Learn proper technique. It will give you an edge over your opponent.

40. A player should try not to have any bad outbursts after missing their shots. This type of reaction builds confidence in your opponents. Your partner will also lose confidence in you.

41. When two right-handed players are playing together, the player facing the net on the left, who has his forehand to the middle of the court, takes the balls on his side of the court plus about 8 to 12 inches across the center line.

42. When two left-handed players are playing together, the player with his forehand toward the center of the court should take any balls on his side of the court plus any ball 8 to 12 inches to the left of center court.

43. When a right-handed and a left-handed player are playing together and both players' backhands are to the middle of the court, the player facing the net on the left side should be considered the forehand and cover his side plus 8 to 12 inches to the right of center court unless both players agree the other player has the stronger backhand.

44. If you like to hit with power and if your opponents cannot recognize when a ball is going out and they hit every ball that they can get their paddles on, then it is to your advantage to have the heavy wind at your back.

45. When your opponents stop hitting you the ball intentionally every time you play, it means your partners are very weak or you

have become a very good player. Feel good about it.

46. There are many styles of play that can be successful in pickleball. You should do things that work for you. Some advanced players have unconventional ways of playing pickleball, and because they have exceptional athletic ability, they are successful more than 50 percent of the time. Beginners with average ability would be more successful if they used conventional tennis strokes and strategy before they pick up bad habits and are unable to change.

47. A player should not be one-dimensional; they should try to develop a complete game of hitting with placement as well as power. Develop a good lob and drop volley as well as a good soft game. A player will not be predictable if he has variety in his pickleball game.

48. If your partner is a much weaker player than you are and your opponents are hitting as many balls as possible to him, then hitting a soft dink into the NVZ is not to your advantage because it gives your opponent more time to hit another ball to your partner.

49. After hitting the ball toward your opponent, follow the same line that the ball is traveling when advancing toward the NVZ line. This will give you a good angle and position for your opponent's return shot.

50. If your team should hit the ball close to the opponent's right sideline and the ball will be a volley or ground stroke then you and your partner should divide the court into three equal thirds when you are waiting at the NVZ line for the return. The player on the right side of the court protects his sideline and the right third of the court. The other player protects the middle third of the court and you leave the far left third of the court open. Your opponent may try to hit a sharp crosscourt shot to the open space, but such a crosscourt shot is difficult. Most players cannot make this shot consistently, so seek to protect the two-thirds of the court near the ball location, and especially the center lane, and you will win many more points than you lose.

12 Reasons Why You May Have Lost the Point

1. I hit the ball too high and not at my opponent's toes.
2. I did not aim my shoulder and the face of the paddle motionless at my target before I made contact with the ball.
3. I did not split step early enough. I was still moving at the point of contact of my opponent's hit.
4. I was in no man's land and not one inch from the NVZ line, which exposed my feet to a tough low shot.
5. I did not step back one and a half feet behind the baseline after I served and missed the third hit because the ball landed at my toes.
6. I did not give myself enough margin for error on my shot.
7. I hit the ball too fast and too deep to allow me to be accurate and consistent.
8. I forgot which direction the wind was blowing and did not play the wind.
9. I hit an opponent's ball that was going out of bounds. Why didn't I predict this? The wind was at his back, the contact point was below the net, and his swing was really fast.
10. I tried and missed a low percentage angle shot rather than waiting for a high percentage shot down the middle of the court to the left opponent's left foot.
11. I did not watch the ball hit my paddle or make a sound at the moment of contact. Instead, I looked up too soon and mis-hit the ball.
12. I hit the return of serve shot too fast to allow me to get to the NVZ line before the serving team returned my shot through the open net position. As a consequence, my shot got returned to my feet.

Coach Mo's Best Clichés

1. What's the most important thing you can do to win? Pick a great partner!

2. What are two of the most important concepts needed for winning? Patience and leeway for error.
3. The game is just an extension of practice.
4. Placement is more important than power.
5. Give your opponents a chance to lose. Patience is a virtue. Work the point.
6. The team with the least unforced errors usually wins.
7. Your fastest shot up high is not as good as your slowest shot at your opponent's toes. Every ball you hit should be aimed at your opponent's toes, preferably to their backhand.
8. The faster that you hit the ball the faster you must split step into your ready position.
9. Win the point at the NVZ line, not from the baseline, because a net man playing volleys will beat a deep man playing ground strokes 90 percent of the time.
10. Do not try to hit a winner off of a very fast difficult shot. Instead, keep it in play and block it down the middle and low.
11. Only hit the ball as fast as you can be accurate and consistent.
12. The better that you get, the harder it is to win because no one will hit the ball to you, so pick a great partner.
13. A good volleyer uses good bowling technique. A bowler first pauses to aim the ball at his target, then steps toward his target, and then follows through toward his target.
14. Whenever possible pause to aim (set the proper angle and direction of the face of your paddle), step, and finish toward your target. Do not rush or guess. Instead, aim!
15. Do not sacrifice being balanced and ready in an attempt to gain a better position on the court.

Play Pickleball Like a Smart Boxer

1. A boxer always jabs with his left hand, waiting patiently for an opening to make a powerful swinging knockout punch with his right hand.

2. A pickleball player should jab at his volleys (extension at the elbow joint with a firm wrist), waiting patiently for the ball to be the proper height (12 inches or higher above the net), and the proper speed (not too fast), before hitting a knockout swinging volley shot.

If a boxer used his powerful right hand too often he would probably be knocked out cold. The same thing applies to a pickleball player who does not work the point with his jab volley, waiting for the proper time for a swinging volley.

How to Become a Complete Pickleball Player

1. Place all shots low to opponents' feet.
2. Keep the ball down the middle 80 percent of the time.
3. Placement is more important than power.
4. Have patience and work the point.
5. Keep proper court position, stay linked to your partner, and cover the high percentage area of the court.
6. Learn efficient footwork. Learn when to shuffle step, when to split step, when to side step, and when to cross step.
7. In selecting shots, use high percentage shots (low and down the middle) and avoid low percentage shots (angled toward sidelines).
8. Allow a margin for error for all shots.
9. Play the wind. Keep it on your mind at all times.
10. Learn good stroke techniques.
11. Reduce your unforced errors.
12. Learn how to recognize your opponents' out balls as soon as they make contact with the ball.
13. Make a mental book on your opponents and on your own strengths and weaknesses.
14. Develop good shot anticipation. Learn to read the shoulder, feet, and paddle face indications of your opponent.
15. Value and participate in practice. The game should become an extension of practice.

GLOSSARY & DEFINITIONS

3/4 Winner: Not hitting a shot the fastest that you are capable of hitting so you will not sacrifice placement for power.

Backhand: Hitting the ball on the left side of your body for right-handed players and the opposite for left-hand players.

Closed Paddle Face: A paddle face with the hitting side angled downward, toward the opponent court surface. The closed face is used for downward hits such as the overhead smash.

Continental Grip: The point of the V between your thumb and index finger is placed at the middle of the top of the handle when your paddle is perpendicular to the ground.

Cross Step: From a split step position, moving your right foot toward the left post or left foot toward the right post without moving your other foot at all.

Crosscourt shot: Hitting the ball diagonally into the opponent's court.

Dink: A very soft shot designed to bounce in or very near the kitchen. When all players are fully forward, soft, unattackable dink shots that bounce in the kitchen area are often the smartest and safest shots to play.

Drop Volley: A softly hit ball that is placed just over the net with an under spin so it won't bounce high.

Forehand: Hitting the ball on the right side of your body for right-handed players and the opposite for left-hand players.

Ground Stroke: A ball that is hit after it bounces.

Half Volley (hitting on the short hop): A groundstroke shot made immediately after a bounce.

Lob: A ball that is hit over your opponent's head and bounces inside the baseline.

Non-Volley Zone (NVZ or Kitchen) " The area of the court between the net and the front edge of the serving boxes.

No Man's Land: The area between the kitchen and the baseline, where a player is most vulnerable.

Open Paddle Face: A paddle face tilted back past perpendicular so that its hitting side looks upward, toward the sky, rather than straight ahead. The upward tilt (open paddle face) provides lift to help carry the ball over the net.

Overhead: A ball hit with the center of the paddle from a point as high as you can reach over your head.

Poach: When a player cuts in front of his partner to take his shot.

Pure Winner: When your opponent never even touches your shot.

Put-Away: Offensive shot to try to end the point with no hope of a return.

Rolling the Ball: Brushing upwards on the ball, applying topspin or "roll forward" spin, causing the ball to roll forward and swerve downward so as to help it stay in bounds.

Split Step: A compressed ready position where the feet are parallel and ready to spring toward the required direction. It's a footwork technique in which a player does a small bounce on both feet, just as the opponent hits the ball. This lets the player move more quickly in either direction.

Top Spin: Comes from brushing upwards on the ball, thus making the ball rotate forward as it is moving. Topspin on a ball causes the ball to dive or drop, thus tending to hold the shot in bounds. Topspin is the opposite of backspin.

Under-spin or Backspin: Comes from brushing under the ball, thus making the ball rotate backwards as it is moving. Under-spin on a ball causes the ball to stay up or "float."

Unforced Error: A shot error that cannot be attributed to any factor other than poor judgment and execution by the player.

Volley: A ball that is hit before it touches the ground.

ABOUT THE AUTHORS

Richard Movsessian (Coach Mo)

Richard Movsessian, a.k.a. "Coach Mo," received his B.S. degree in Physical Education and a Masters of Education from Boston University. He taught physical education in Massachusetts for 29 years. He coached high school varsity tennis for 13 years and was voted coach of the year in 1979. After retiring from teaching, he became a USATA-certified teaching pro, providing private tennis lessons. He played on the 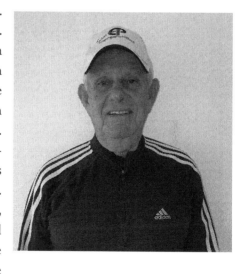 1996 USATA 4.5 Florida State Championship tennis team. After taking up pickleball, Coach Mo taught over 20,000 students during free clinics that have continued for nearly 20 years. He was honored by The Villages, Florida, in 2015 with a commemorative paddle. In 2010, Coach Mo, at the age of 70, and his partner, Phil Bagley, were the 35+ open men's doubles silver medal winners at the USAPA National Championship held in Buckeye, Arizona. Coach Mo has also traveled extensively teaching clinics. Coach Mo received an honorary membership to the new International Pickleball Teaching Professional Association (IPTPA) and was asked to speak at the first IPTPA World Congress meeting.

Coach Mo has sold over 7,000 pickleball instructional DVDs. He operates the web site www.pickleballcoach.com, which contains a wealth of free helpful instructional information.

Joe Baker (Video Joe)

His pickleball buddies call him "Video Joe" because of his many YouTube instructional videos and because he is always video recording local tournaments. Joe Baker received his B.S. degree in Mechanical Engineering from North Carolina State University in 1980. He retired from the DuPont Corporation after 35 years of service. Joe received much of his pickleball training from Coach Mo. He is the silver medal winner in the 2016 Richmond, Virginia, Senior Games advanced (4.0+) men's doubles division and the 2017 silver medal winner at the Virginia State Senior Games 60–64 men's open doubles division. Joe is most known for his YouTube pickleball instructional videos, which have been watched by more than a half million viewers. His hobby is breaking down and analyzing pickleball tournament video recordings to determine which shots and strategies work and which do not. From this, he's developed predictive statistics and optimal playing strategies. Joe is the author of *At the Line Pickleball: The Winning Doubles Pickleball Strategy*. Learn more at www.pickleballhelp.blogspot.com.

Made in the USA
San Bernardino, CA
10 January 2020